MW01200187

ALL THE PARTS WE EXILE

All the Parts We Exile

A Memoir

Roza Nozari

Alfred A. Knopf Canada

PUBLISHED BY ALFRED A. KNOPF CANADA

Content warning: This book includes references to sexual violence, harassment, and physical, psychological and financial abuse.

Note from the author: Names and descriptions of some people have been changed to protect their identities. In rare instances where further anonymity was needed, I have turned one person or place into two. I have made every effort to ensure these changes did not disturb the truthfulness of the events recounted.

Knopf Canada
Penguin Random House Canada
320 Front Street West, Suite 1400
Toronto Ontario, M5V 3B6, Canada
penguinrandomhouse.ca

The authorized representative in the EU for product safety and compliance is Penguin Random House Ireland, Morrison Chambers, 32 Nassau Street, Dublin D02 YH68, Ireland, https://eu-contact.penguin.ie

LIBRARY AND ARCHIVES CANADA CATALOGUING IN PUBLICATION
Title: All the parts we exile / Roza Nozari.
Names: Nozari, Roza, author.
Identifiers: Canadiana (print) 20240391705 | Canadiana (ebook) 20240396200 |
ISBN 9781039007062 (hardcover) | ISBN 9781039007031 (EPUB)
Subjects: LCSH: Nozari, Roza. | LCSH: Muslim sexual minorities—Canada—Biography. |
LCSH: Mothers and daughters—Canada—Biography. | LCSH: Iranians—Canada—
Biography. | LCSH: Illustrators—Canada—Biography. | LCSH: Self-acceptance. | CSH:
Iranian Canadian women—Biography. | LCGFT: Autobiographies.
Classification: LCC HQ75.4.N69 A3 2025 | DDC 306.76/63092—dc23

Book design: Lisa Jager
Cover image and interior illustrations: Roza Nozari
Typeset by: Erin Cooper

Printed in the United States of America

1st Printing

Penguin
Random House
KNOPF CANADA

For my mother and my sisters

For Story, Storm, Jacob and Micah

"I will have my serpent's tongue—my woman's voice, my sexual voice, my poet's voice. I will overcome the tradition of silence."

—GLORIA E. ANZALDÚA, *Borderlands*

1

DEPARTURES

I was desperate to leave my sister's house. At twenty-six, I'd been living in Yara's basement in a suburb of Toronto for the past two years. Mom was newly separated from her second husband and planned on moving in, too. I couldn't get the visual of us sharing a five-by-four-metre room in the basement out of my head. Cohabitating like partners, bickering over her loud snoring or my tendency to leave candy wrappers around.

I also couldn't bear to have Yara, the responsible eldest daughter, take care of not one, but two grown adults in the family. She had a habit of taking us in, if any of us were short on money, or needing a place to stay. When Mom started asking incessantly if we could get a two-bedroom together, I started panic-reviewing listings on the internet for myself.

The salmon-toned triplex I found in the queer online ads was tucked onto a tree-lined street, cars parked bumper to bumper and middle-class couples decked out in athleisure speed-walking their dogs. A five-minute walk away, you'd find yourself in old Chinatown. Little bakeries selling coconut buns and red bean sesame balls next to modern thrift stores and coffee shops.

The apartment was a maximalist's dream. Ornate couches thrifted from garage sales, gold-framed art busily scattered across the walls and giant windows to let in the sun. The person living there was interested in keeping the home queer. When I heard the rent was $600, I asked how quickly I could move in, half-jokingly.

Five days before moving into my first Toronto apartment, I invited Mom to come with me to see the place. Fifteen minutes into the drive, she was already complaining that the apartment was too far away and that it would be difficult for her to get to me. As we arrived and walked up the driveway, I noticed her glaring at the building's peeling paint. Hoping for her blessing, I quickly tried to steer her in a positive direction: "It's so cute, right! Pink! It's a pink house!"

I could feel there was finality to this transition, and maybe on some level, she could, too. Having just finished graduate school, I was launching myself into a social work career. No more returning to Yara's. The practical benefits of free room and board had often outweighed my desire for independence. This time it wasn't a desire for independence, though; it was an uncompromising need. Like if I stayed, I would fall into a chaotic existential crisis that would culminate in some sort of death of self. Or worse, I'd land in a Freudian nightmare with an Oedipal mother, smothering me into a regressive state— forever her baby.

We walked up the stairs of the triplex, Mom remarking on how filthy the carpet was. "But I won't be sleeping here, right?" I chuckled awkwardly, trying to soften her stern face.

I walked first into the apartment, guiding her past a stuffed clothing rack in a narrow hallway. Mom took off her shoes and I led her into the bedroom directly in front of the door. Immediately, her hesitation transmuted into anger.

"Oh my god." Her eyes widened. "You're not moving here."

"It's not that bad, Mom."

"Oh my god, the carpets!" She slapped her hand against her cheek. "The carpets!" she exclaimed again, in English, pretending to faint. It was rare for her to speak English unless it was to punctuate a moment like this, which worked well because much of her English vocabulary came from watching soap operas.

Admittedly, while the living room was beautiful, this room was in pretty terrible shape. There was a giant blood-stain on the mattress, dark tire tracks across the ceiling, and a beige carpet that looked like it had never been cleaned. Even then, I wasn't going to let Mom know that I knew how bad the room was. It was $600 a month—and to me, its character made up for its flaws.

Mom looked up at the ceiling, then down at the carpet, and shuddered. "You're going to need a Persian rug for these floors," she muttered. She continued onward to the living room, where my soon-to-be roommate and their friend were assembling a table. Pieces of wood were scattered across the floor, blocking our entry. "Who is this man?" she whispered to me in Farsi. Mom immediately backed up and bee-lined to the door. I mouthed the word *sorry* to my soon-to-be-roommate and followed her out, embarrassed by her behaviour.

The whole way back to the car and back home, Mom repeated the word *no*. At some point, I wondered if she'd forgotten her mouth was still saying *no*. I sat silently, listening to her weave between *no* and rants about how we didn't come all the way to this country to have her university-educated daughter with graduate degrees move into a dirty apartment in the city with roommates. "You'll wait until something better comes," she declared.

I was familiar with this part of Mom. A dragon whose fiery breath would, at best, push me away, and at worse, burn me. At other times, a snake, wrapping its body around me, not noticing my constricted, slowing breath. In moments like these, my frustration was also blended with curiosity about where it all came from. I had become acutely aware that my mother had lived a life before me, and whatever had existed there continued to haunt her well into her fifties. Its cold, blue claw would suddenly zombie its way into her body. A possession of sorts that left me disoriented. Like, where did my mother—the kind, empathetic, curious one—go when the dragon in her arose?

My family emigrated to Canada before I was born, and what I knew of what preceded me—and what had shaped my mother—came in bits and pieces that I had to pry out and probe for. Mom was mostly tight-lipped about her past. From the timeline I'd stitched together, I knew that they left Iran in 1990, a couple years after the war between Iran and Iraq had officially ended.

The simplified version is that in the aftermath of the 1979 Revolution, the Shah was ousted and the Islamic regime took over, newly governing the country with a restrictive, conservative version of Islamic law. With the establishment of surveillance forces like the morality police, women's rights were deteriorating quickly—from their right to vote to their autonomy over how they dressed and behaved in public. Watching rights being stripped away, my parents wondered what future was possible for themselves and their daughters. Beyond that, with such little work coming their way, they wondered if there was more opportunity elsewhere.

The move itself was where the details thinned. In September of 1990, they were living in Esfahan, a city in the centre of Iran, where they'd both grown up. My father was a truck driver; Mom stayed home, raising Yara and Yasaman, who were nine and eight at the time of leaving. With hopes of ensuring a safe future for their children, they decided to travel to Turkey, and from Turkey, made their way to Canada, where they claimed asylum. The lack of emotion and detail when Mom told the story always left me unsatisfied, striving for something more with a barrage of questions. Perhaps I knew that there was more to the story than what she shared.

Six months after the move, Mom was pregnant with me. Her yearning for her family and home deepened in ways that felt like quicksand. The more she thought of them, the more she sank into an unrelenting ache. Memories of the last time she was pregnant flooded her. Her last pregnancy was Yasaman, when she was rushed to the hospital two months early. Worried about whether Yasaman would survive, her mother stood by her hospital bed, stroking her hair and reminding her to breathe. Her father, her sisters, her brothers, her nephews and nieces, aunts and uncles crowded the hospital halls, praying and waiting for news about the baby. There was love there—so much of it. Terrified, her mother cradled her until eventually, Yasaman was born—five pounds small, but alive and healthy.

When it was time for my birth, Mom lay in the hospital bed, missing her mother even more than usual. There was no one to cradle her face and tell her things would be okay. No one praying for her in the hallways. Instead, a doctor and nurse stood at her bedside, along with a new friend she had made on her first day in Canada, at a shelter. The couple months of welfare-mandated ESL had done little to improve her English. She lay there, blankly staring at them, unsure of what was being said.

My mother recalls my father waiting outside as she went into labour. When they handed me to her, she laid my seven-pound body to her chest, suddenly feeling less alone in her world. Her eyes traced my face, enamoured by the peach fuzz on my skin, my wrinkles and full head of hair. She felt like her heart had been cracked open and out of it gushed more and more love.

"You were easy," Mom explained to me. "You were always so easy." It was hard to reconcile the story she was telling me with the word *easy*. "You know, it's okay if I wasn't," I've responded numerous times. Still, she clung to that story.

My father joined her briefly in her hospital room before returning to my sisters, who were sleeping at home. Mom pleaded with him to return first thing in the morning, and he promised he would as he rushed out the door.

When the nurses peeled me off her body and carried me away, Mom felt a sudden surge of panic, her eyes darting between the nurses wrapping my body in cloth and the door. She tried to understand why they would take me away, speaking in the few words she knew. My name had become one of the few shared words she could use to communicate. "Roza," she repeated, gesturing at the door. "Roza," she repeated, louder and with more urgency. When words failed, she hobbled over to the door and attempted to walk down the hallway, trying to find me. Realizing that I was the only one that could soothe my mother, the nurses returned me to her arms, leaving me with her overnight. "I didn't want to be away from you—not for one second," Mom reminded me.

Bright and early the next morning, Mom slowly changed into the clothes she, herself, had neatly packed into her overnight bag. After being discharged, she tucked me into her arms and waited alone in a chair by the hospital entrance, her baby bag down by her feet. She sat in this chair for hours, waiting, watching as families carried their newborn babies to the car. The nurses would huddle together at the nursing station, watching her with worry in their eyes. Sometimes, they would point at the phone and she would shake her head and stare down at her feet, ashamed to be attracting attention. Eventually, her brave face faded into sadness. Rocking me back and forth, she tried not to make eye contact with the nurses, who were still staring with pity as she cried. Five hours later, my father pulled up to the hospital doors, where my mother was still seated. "My friend's car broke down and he needed my help," he explained, defensively. Deflated and exhausted, Mom hobbled out to the car quietly—one hand carrying me, one hand carrying her bag.

These glimpses of the life my mother lived before me and in my early years were rare, but always revealing of the things that continued to haunt her and our relationship now. Here, it revealed a birth story that was as much about devastating loss as it was about joy. A story that I imagine is shared beyond us. How many of us were grown in a body that aches for home, just as it gifts us a home. Our growing bodies absorbing the earthquake of their grief. Our mothers, feeling alone. The ones who simultaneously experienced the happiness of their baby's arrival and the painful absence of those who were *not* there to hold them through it. Mothers who yearn for their mothers as they prepare to mother us.

As I prepared to move out to my first apartment in Toronto and discover the independence I so craved, my mother's grasping hands felt familiar. To me, they were emblematic of the inescapable truth about us: that just as there is profound joy in our relationship, there is an immense amount of grief. Between us, grief was like the sun, and joy, the moon. My mother preferred looking at the moon, especially at its fullest. The sun would burn the eyes. Yet like the sun, grief was there in our morning sky, whether we looked at it or not. Grief that is hers, that is mine, that is ours, that is historical and collective. Grief that has shaped our relationship and our very personhood, just as joy has. And the more we fervently attempt to avert our eyes and exile the grief, to banish our histories and the selves we once were to the skies, the further we drift away from each other.

This is a story of bringing to light historical and personal truths; of finding a new familial closeness; of owning our pasts and accepting the people we've been to become who we really are. It's a story of exile and of love.

2

APPETITES

My mom's voice boomed across the apartment when she was on the phone. "Who is it? Who is it?" I asked eagerly as she waved me away with her hands. Her voice itself was a gossip, telling me whether she was talking to someone from back home or someone here. When the volume rose, my sisters would joke that she was literally yelling across an ocean. I started going down the long list of people it could be on the other side of the call. Could be someone on my mother's side. One of two grandparents, three aunties, two uncles and too many cousins to count. Or perhaps, my father's side, who called far less often— three aunties, four uncles and a handful of cousins. "*Khanoom*," my mom whispered at me, covering the phone. *Khanoom* was a Farsi word for "lady" or "Ms." It was what we lovingly called my grandmother.

A few minutes into the phone call, she pointed the phone at us kids, lounging on the couch. Yasaman was seventeen at the time, Yara was eighteen, and I was eight. Yasaman bolted immediately. Mom's eyes widened towards her as she walked away, a quiet cue to say *You're being disrespectful.* Regardless, she disappeared, seeking refuge in her room from Mom's badgering. Yara aggressively mouthed the word *no!* and refocused on the television. Mom eagerly pressed the phone against my ear instead. "*Salaam!*" I said, loudly, into the speaker. Mom mouthed the words I was supposed to say after that. "*Khoobi?*" she whispered, meaning, "How are you?" I parroted back the words, trying my best to mimic her intonations and double-consonant sounds. "*Mashallah, mashallah!*" my grandmother responded, excited by every word I spoke.

The more I spoke Farsi, the more those on the other side of the phone gushed over me, as did my mom. Somehow, I managed to carve out an accent so unique, it was charming and comical to them. I flattened my *r*'s the way Canadians did. I stretched out my words and rhythmically spoke the way Iranians from our city, Esfahan, did. It wasn't known to be an elegant accent like that of people from Tehran, but it was one that I loved. Mostly because it was what Mom and I shared, and my efforts endeared me to her endlessly.

My father took the phone next, speaking just as loudly as Mom. "These kids, they're not human anymore, you know? They're Canadian now," he chuckled into the receiver. Yara rolled her eyes, a common response between her and Yasaman to Dad's commentary. He smiled and winked at me as if to reassure me—*the others, not you*. I was somewhat of a kiss-ass, enjoying the moments where my parents shone their approval on me rather than on my sisters.

There was no denying that Yasaman and Yara were distancing themselves—from the family, from our culture, our roots. They were nine and ten years older than me, respectively, and in an entirely different stage of life. Teens who were trying to figure themselves out in a place our parents hadn't grown up in. They'd known a different, harsher version of our father, but it took me a while to understand that.

Yasaman was the middle child in our family, with a complexion so fair, many confused her for a Caucasian kid. We were sisters but there was nothing that felt connective about our faces, our bodies, our skin or our personalities. I marvelled at how effortlessly cool came to her. Yasaman's signature look was to pull her lush curls into a ponytail and frame her face with two long strands of hair. Though my parents generally disapproved of her fashion choices, they eventually gave in, letting her dress like the other local girls in plaid miniskirts or hip-hugging jeans and cropped button-downs. Even if Mom had firmly disapproved, Yasaman would have done what she wanted anyway. Not even Mom could win in a fight with Yasaman, so no one tried.

Yara was the eldest, and the more responsible sibling. She worked a part-time job at a bakery to help my parents with rent, and rarely complained. There was a generosity and sense of duty in Yara's spirit. She and I were the most similar in appearance. Childhood photos of Yara looked so similar to me that I sometimes thought it *was* me. In some ways, I wanted to be her. We both had almond-shaped eyes, though mine were thinner, like Dad's, and olive skin, though I was a couple shades darker.

The two of them rarely spoke about Iran, if at all. Outside of knowing her family members, Yara's only memory of Iran was of the home they'd lived in during the Iran–Iraq War. Yasaman, on the contrary, even though she was a year younger, held detailed memories of the things that had happened there, sometimes sharing them in random moments to everyone's surprise. Like the wedding shop near my grandparents' house from when she was in grades one and two. Around the corner and up a set of stairs. Mom would occasionally walk her inside, knowing how much she loved staring up at the window from outside at the beautiful dresses on display.

There were only one or two photos of Yasaman as a baby and none of her childhood, whereas there were a handful of Yara as a baby and albums full of me at every year. I felt sadness for Yasaman, knowing how important those photos were to me. The reasons for it varied over time—a combination of her having been born during the war and of Mom having her hands full with two children, one year apart. Either way, Yasaman never showed that it bothered her much, only pointing to it as a comedic punchline. In retrospect, perhaps it was too vulnerable to point to with honesty. Yasaman's humour had become an armouring of sorts. A less vulnerable way to point at something painful that probably *did* bother her.

What I knew of Yasaman during those years was that she was a self-proclaimed troublemaker, often up to mischief around the neighbourhood. When Mom recalled memories of Yasaman, it was with an exhausted sigh. Mom would repeat: "She was always a difficult child, always being naughty." Yara was the opposite—a very reserved, studious and sensitive child, whose only flaw was how often she cried. But that changed as she grew older and took on more responsibility for our family— rarely did I see her in tears.

After the phone call, Mom went back into the kitchen. Her fingers were soon stamped with the orange of saffron, the sweet and salty air of the rice and lamb stew filling the room. All morning, she had been gently cleaning and picking apart *sabzi* (herbs), one piece of parsley at a time. Sometimes, I looked over to see her in a meditative state, focused on the task. At other times, she looked transported elsewhere, her eyes dazed and distant. After a minute, she would exhale and say, "*Yadesh bekhair*," an Iranian phrase one says when they're reminded of a pleasant memory. The phrase always carried a sense of nostalgia.

When she opened the cabinet doors and pulled out the *robe anar* (pomegranate syrup), I dragged a chair next to the bubbling pots and stood atop, waiting for the inevitable moment she would offer me a spoonful.

"What's this called?" I asked, pointing to the sticky bottle.

"*Robe anar*," she responded, emphasizing the short rolled *r*'s.

I craved the tart sweetness of the syrup and waited for her to leave the kitchen before taking a few swigs straight from the bottle.

There were no timers, no measuring cups and no cooking lessons when Mom was in the kitchen. When the rice was done, she placed a tray atop the pot and flipped it upside down, revealing *tahdig*—the crispy brown bottom of the dish. In this home, there was nothing mundane about the act of cooking. The layering of herbs and spices, the blending of sweet and tangy flavours, the slow process of simmering stew, the bejewelling of rice. It was enchanting.

The kitchen was where we found a way to speak to each other about home, without really talking about home. It was where a child like me, with no tangible memory or experience of Iran, could find a way of knowing it. The tongue, trying to find a way to gently roll the *r* of *anar*. Wrapping itself around the stew's softened split peas and tender lamb, savouring a meal the way my mother once did with her mother. My connection to a place I'd never been was a question that baffled everyone in the family, especially in light of my sisters' growing distance from it all.

Where Yara, Yasaman and Mom shared the experience of home and migration, Mom and I were bonded by our appetites.

"Do you remember when you ate a whole fish?" Mom nudged me as she stirred the *gheimeh* (split lentil and lamb stew). She had spent hours and hours in the kitchen with me by her side, making one of my favourites: *mahi polo*. The rice was beautiful in its shades of green, and the smell of dill filled our apartment. The fish was fried to perfection, a yellow crisp on the outside skin from the turmeric. She had made a platter for the family and left it on the kitchen table. Alone with the food, I climbed up on a chair and began eating uncontrollably with my hands, straight out of the platter. By the time Mom came back, most of it was gone. She chuckled as she retold me the story. "Even then," she whispered to me, "I wasn't angry at you." Instead, she said she'd walked into the kitchen and paused in shock, her eyes making sense of the nearly empty tray before erupting into laughter. "*Shekamoo*," she called me—a sweet name you would call a child with a big appetite.

When my family moved to Canada in the early nineties, there were many things my mom didn't know—like how to ride the subway, or where to find dried limes. The fact that she and my sisters knew so few English words made it even harder. Mom knew the words *Refoogee Aseelum* because my father told her to practise the words again and again on the airplane over. She knew *hello*, *yes*, and *no*.

When the social worker at the welfare office assigned my pregnant mother mandatory English as a Second Language classes, she was delighted. The idea of relying less on my father was appealing to her. Dad was excused from the mandatory classes because he knew more of the language and someone had to make money for rent. Mom eagerly signed up for classes at an east-end Toronto public school, thirty minutes away from the one-bedroom apartment they were renting.

As they saved up for a car of their own, Dad taught Mom how to ride public transportation. Together, they waited at the top of the street, beside the red-and-white pole marked with numbers. He guided her onto the bus and pointed at the square box by the driver, where she was to insert her token.

After a few days, Mom started riding the bus on her own. She left Yasaman and Yara at home—eight and nine years old—trusting that they could walk themselves to school and back on their own, much like they'd done in Esfahan. Mom would sit at a seat near the front and gaze out the window, searching for people who looked like her family. She missed them fiercely. *That man's eyes look like Shahin's eyes*, she would tell herself—quietly finding her brothers and sisters in the faces of strangers. She looked for her father, *Baba Ali*—his silver-streaked hair, his curved nose, his crisp suit jackets. Her mother, too—her petite frame and her olive, freckled skin and paper-thin lips. It was an ache that rarely dulled, rarely quieted.

To Mom's surprise, most of the ESL students were other young Iranian women who, like her, barely spoke English. During lunch, they would open their plastic containers to homemade meals that smelled of Iran; the scent of herbs from *ghormeh sabzi*—cilantro, chives, parsley—would waft around the room. The sweet smell of saffron, the fragrant dill in *sabzi polo*, an herbaceous rice.

Fariba, one of the students, opened her threading business for two dollars a pop every day during the lunch hour. With very little money in their pockets, the women excitedly crowded the school washroom, each taking a seat in Fariba's "spa." Over time, going to class would feel like visiting friends. Briefly, these friendships dulled the longing they all felt for family back home.

Eventually, Mom's social worker realized she had been leaving her children at home unattended, as she'd done in Iran, and so she was no longer allowed to go to class. A few months later, I was born.

The women Mom met in those classes led her to more women. Eventually, I would know these women as aunties, who we referred to as "Khaleh." Over time my mother carved out a chosen family for herself with five or six other families. Connected not by blood like my aunties back home, but by migration stories and homeland ties. Like us, most had arrived in Canada without any other family beyond their husbands and kids.

By the time I was eight, they were a regular part of our lives—more so than my father, who was rarely home. As a truck driver, he was often away for two weeks at a time, returning for a day or two before being sent off again. On any given weekend, whether he was home or not, the families would come together for lunch or dinner. One night, an auntie called my mom, inviting her to a picnic.

"Leslie Park? Okay, we'll come, too," Mom responded, nodding joyfully as I eagerly asked when. Early the next morning, Mom was already up and loading the car with half our refrigerator neatly packaged into bags. She cracked open and sliced a watermelon, her hand reaching towards me with a piece.

"Are Yara and Yasaman coming?"

"No—just us."

When we arrived at the park, the car in front of us was blasting Persian music, and we could see the people in it dancing and singing through the window. We upped the volume of our own music and pulled up next to them, dancing and singing back. We parked near a big spread of picnic blankets alongside a few other cars, and everyone began arranging food onto a giant spread of picnic blankets.

Ground beef, chicken thighs and halved tomatoes marinated on long metal skewers, wrapped in foil. Bags of pita bread, fresh from the Arab grocery store we all frequented. Sliced onions, fresh radishes and sprigs of parsley. Persian salami—halal and pork-free. Containers of watermelon and cut-up cantaloupe. A Thermos of Ahmad Tea. Stacks of cups and plates. Bags of pistachios, sunflower seeds and nuts.

On one side, some of the men sat in circles, playing cards and backgammon. Others had started barbecuing the food.

The women sat together on the other side, their laughter booming. The kids played soccer, or cards. I was envious of the kids who could speak Farsi in ways that I couldn't and who had memories of homes in Iran, of their extended families. I knew home in pieces—through the phone calls and the few photographs. Through the memories shared by Mom, or by the other women at these picnics.

I unequivocally defined home as Iran back then, never considering Canada my home. Home was where your family was from, where your roots lived, where your lineage could be traced back to—not necessarily where you lived now. It didn't feel strange to think this way. Having grown up in Scarborough, a racialized neighbourhood east of Toronto, most of the other kids in my classes identified home in similar ways—as where their families came from, regardless of their place of birth. Rarely did anyone identify as Canadian, unless they were white.

I sat next to Mom, who split sunflower shells between her teeth and handed me the inside seed. The women would reminisce about the gatherings they would have with their own families—their visits to villas in the north of Iran, where thirty or forty of them would load up their cars with six or seven people, music blasting and dancing all the way there. Or how the figs here could never compare to the juicy figs back home. One after another, the women would riff off of each other, glowing as they shared story after story and laughed about how different things were here.

"Mom, how many cousins do I have?"

"A lot—over twenty." She smiled, and my eyes widened.

My whole body buzzed with excitement as I listened to their stories, each one like a spoonful of pomegranate kernels I held in my mouth, savouring their sweet and tangy flavour and wanting more. Their stories brought me closer and closer to knowing Iran—to knowing home. Though I was encouraged several times to go off and play with the other kids, I kept returning to the circle of women, slowly nibbling on watermelon and listening in. Quietly, I sat near my mother, fantasizing about the fruit trees, the road trips and the family I would one day meet.

3

ARMOUR

With my father on the road for weeks at a time, my mother was a hawk with us. Often perched by the window of our sixth-floor apartment, she would watch for our return from school.

Mom was there for most of the school year, though from late spring to mid-fall, she worked a seasonal job at a garment factory. It was mostly immigrant women like herself, working as packers, folding and packaging clothing for shipment. When she wasn't there, it was Yara and Yasaman who would keep an eye out for me and each other.

As Mom garnered more community with other Iranian women, she was hearing more stories about violence, amplified by the local news. Paul Bernardo, dubbed the Scarborough Rapist, and Karla Homolka, his wife at the time, were particularly talked about during her early years in Canada. Reportedly, Bernardo had raped and/or murdered at least eighteen women and girls between 1987 and 1992, ranging from fourteen to twenty-two years old, some of which, allegedly, had occurred alongside Homolka. Homolka struck a plea bargain and served prison time for two counts of manslaughter, whereas Bernardo was sentenced to life imprisonment. Horrified by the violence and loss of life, my mother felt no more at ease knowing he was behind bars.

To Mom, it wasn't that Scarborough, specifically, was unsafe; it was that this country was unsafe, particularly for her daughters. These were distinctions that I understood from a young age, seeing Mom's trust in other mothers in the neighbourhood, permitting us to spend time at our friends' homes, usually in adjacent buildings.

Mom had chosen to move to Scarborough, believing it to be safer than other affordable communities in the area. Our apartment building was concentrated with low-income immigrant families like us. Whatever floor you found yourself on, you would find the smell of curries and incense. We kids spent the summers in the public pool, or hanging off the monkey bars in our parks, or at each other's homes, knowing that we would be fed, watched and well taken care of. That, our mothers could trust.

Some days, with four quarters in my pocket, I was allowed to walk across the parking lot in front of our building to the plaza with the convenience store. Mom, of course, watched from the window. The choice was always obvious and quick: either a mystery grab bag of different candies or a few sour keys. Other kids were there, too. Siblings taking the younger ones and emptying their pockets of nickels and dimes at the cash register. The owner, a Korean man in his forties, was always patient with us kids, helping us count it out—nickel, five; plus a dime, fifteen.

My favourite days were spent at the apartment's pool, just next to our park. Since it was visible from our window, I was allowed to walk myself there and join the other kids, and their parents, who would inevitably crowd the pool during the summers. Mostly, I spent the months reading a scandalous book about teenage romance, feeling slightly rebellious for my garage-sale find. Hours later, my mother would find me still there, skin burnt because I had forgotten to apply sunscreen again, and haul me back home for dinner.

Though we felt a sense of community in Scarborough, it still didn't provide the same sense of security that my mother had known as a girl. The kind that would've eased my mother's anxieties about raising daughters, essentially on her own, in Canada.

Mom grew up in the sixties and seventies in a neighbourhood in Iran that was insular in a way that felt protective. At the time, the country was ruled by Shah Mohammad Reza Pahlavi, the country's last monarch. Under Shah Pahlavi, women had acquired the right to vote in 1963 and the right to abortion in 1967. Where the legal age of marriage was once thirteen—the age my grandmother and eldest aunt were engaged—it was now eighteen.

According to Mom, Shah Pahlavi was invested in a kind of modernity that my mother always referenced as "rivalling the best—the French, the Americans." "Do you remember the anniversary of the Empire?" she would ask her new friends, their eyes lighting up in the memory. "No one could throw a banquet the way the Shah could. Not the French, not the Americans." The ruins of Persepolis, a desert plot of land, were transformed with lavish tents erected across 160 acres, planted greenery and foliage, fifty thousand songbirds flown in from Europe, 150 tons of food flown in from Paris via the army, and a star-studded international guest list.

Mom's father, Baba Ali, had rushed out to buy a television just so the whole family could watch the broadcast of the banquet. My mom and her siblings, their aunties and uncles and cousins, all circled the television, eyes wide at a scale of luxury they had never seen before. When the Shah arrived on his horse, everyone wept.

Of course, the state of awe in that moment was short-lived, and over time, Mom's family grew frustrated with the Shah's exorbitant spending. Especially as many were struggling with the increased inflation and income inequality, amongst other suspicions of corruption and control.

What my mom remembers fondly of that time was growing up in a neighbourhood where there were always watchful eyes around. "You couldn't leave your home without seeing an auntie or an uncle," who were all neighbours, as were her grandparents.

Late into the night, their house was often overflowing with guests. Her mother would be in the kitchen alongside other women, gossiping about the latest word on the street, cooking and preparing chai. A section would be set up on the ground for grandparents: hot charcoal on the *gheyliun* (hookah), ready to be smoked by the elders. The bar near the kitchen was always restocked with wine and her father's favourite whiskey. Baba Ali would be sitting on the ground, alongside his brothers, cousins and friends, playing poker. Loud and rowdy, with *tomans* and personal cheques stretched across the ground as they jokingly argued over who was most likely to cheat.

Mom and her brother would sneakily find their way to the liquor bar when no one was looking. They would giggle as they stole swigs of vodka, their eyes twitching and their noses scrunched. How could anyone like the taste of rubbing alcohol? They laughed. The unspoken rule amongst the children was that they all had each other's back, no matter what.

The next day, Baba Ali would wake at dawn, wash the alcohol from his mouth (a second time, to be sure), perform *wudu*—a purification ritual before prayer—and proceed to prayer.

At the time, what it meant to be Muslim varied across families and even within families. Baba Ali had always raised the family to be devout Muslims, praying five times a day and observing religiously significant dates.

In her teenage years, Mom was especially intrigued by her brother Shahin's ideas around the Muslim faith. Dayee (Uncle)

Shahin was four years her senior—a passionate personality, always arguing his perspectives on Muslim values to the point of rowdy disagreements amongst the siblings escalating to physical fighting. While Mom was Muslim, too, the fights often broke out when she disagreed with the patriarchal lens he often saw Islam through. Some nights, Baba Ali would tire of Shahin's soapbox speeches and aggression, open the door and kick him out for the night, especially when he would start throwing hands.

The first time Mom heard the pitter-patter of Shahin's steps on the roof, she felt relief, knowing he hadn't gone far. As frustrated as she felt with Shahin's tirades, she still worried about him sleeping outside, sometimes in the cold with no dinner. Quietly, she would pull together some blankets and a few bites of food, climb out the window and hand it to him on the roof. It was their code—having each other's back, protecting each other.

Years later, though Mom was raising her daughters in a radically different environment, the code was still the same. That we would have each other's back—Yara, Yasaman, me and Mom.

During the first couple years in Canada, living in East York, it seemed like Yara and Yasaman could only turn to each other. Mom knew little of the barrage of humiliating events and insults hurled at them, with their home-sewn clothes and their thick accents making them targets at school.

In my twenties and thirties, Yara would occasionally share painful childhood experiences of bullying, always couched in humour. I once reflected that Yasaman, for her part, seemed to recall no painful experiences of bullying, instead remembering herself as always pushing back and standing up for herself.

One memory was particularly seared into Yara's mind. She and Yasaman were playing on a playground swing-set one day, pumping their legs and giggling as they tried to reach higher and higher. It was a rare day when they felt like regular kids with no other thought but that of play. When they got off the swings, Yara noticed a younger white boy stomping towards them. The boy stopped at Yasaman, slapped her flush across the face and stomped away.

Yara stood there frozen, watching Yasaman struggle to keep tears from streaming out her eyes. Embarrassed by her own inaction, Yara promised she would never let that happen again.

By the time my sisters reached high school, they were no longer the vulnerable, bullied kids they once were. They had each developed an effective defence against social threats. Yara had become the popular kid at school, excelling both academically and socially. She had fostered a circle of close friends, each of whom was kind, smart and caring. Together, they played recreational sports, finding joy and building community through softball, field hockey and soccer. With a small frame, big, almond-shaped eyes, long dark wavy hair and olive skin, she was voted by her classmates the most likely to be on the cover of *Vogue* magazine.

Yasaman was still the wildest one of our trio: a quintessential middle sister with the impassioned need to be a pain in my mother's ass. She had continued her childhood rebellion, falling into a tough crowd that often seemed to be in trouble or causing trouble.

Yara and Yasaman would take turns picking me up at school until I was old enough to walk myself home, yet the memories I carry most are those where Yasaman walked me home. Donning her blue-and-white oversized Fila coat, her wide-legged jeans and Reebok shoes, she would wait for me to collect my things and march out the doors.

We would walk ten minutes up the street to our apartment along the plaza sidewalk and speed past the mini grocery store where grown men would hang out at the end of the school day, gawking at little girls and teenagers like my sister. Their eyes narrowed as we approached, their smiles revealing some teeth. Like they were looking at us, but really, they were imagining something else.

"Hello, hello," they would say, their eyes fixed on us. "Very pretty, pretty girl," a common refrain.

Yasaman employed a "fuck off" expression as we approached them. I analyzed it like a mask she invoked against danger. Her jaw, clenched, and her eyes, unblinking and narrowed, staring at the space ahead of us. She wasn't afraid to glare at the men, either, occasionally rolling her eyes. She had more fight in her than the rest of us. At times, it came across as meanness, like when she ridiculed Mom for mispronouncing English words. Other times, when those grown men dared stare at her and call her a pretty girl, her fuck-off face served a greater purpose of protecting us both.

She would pick up our pace and walk us into the alley on the side of the plaza, opening the latch on the metal gate that led to our building's parking lot. I would gaze up to our apartment on the sixth floor, and there my mom would be, where she always was, watching for us from the window.

When Yasaman and Yara graduated high school, they took different paths. Yara enrolled at university and started working more hours to financially support Mom with the apartment. Yasaman, having struggled in high school with learning disabilities, opted for a more hands-on program in community college. Mom hated that Yasaman was going to college instead of university, never mind the late-night hours of the program. The idea of a young woman taking the bus alone from the city centre, an hour away, and returning at night was terrifying. It wasn't what she had wanted for her, but it was what Yasaman wanted for herself.

With their transition came my own as I learned to walk myself home after school. Now, older, I had picked up my own safety mechanisms, choosing to walk home behind others from my apartment building, or walk the alley only when there were others near. Some days, I even made friends, like a young Afghan girl who had newly started wearing a hijab to hide a terrible haircut. I was no less scared than before, but with each walk, I grew braver.

Yasaman's transition to public transit downtown intensified Mom's anxiety, even though Yasaman, herself, felt relatively relaxed about the whole thing. One particular evening in the winter, Yasaman was on the bus home from college; it was busy as usual, a mixture of students and working-class folks. As the bus emptied out, she felt the hot gaze of someone glaring at her. Her body stiffened, sensing she'd had the misfortune of becoming someone's object of fascination. She panned right, slow enough to catch his face, fast enough to forget it. Slumped into a seat was an older, plump white man in his fifties. A smirk flashed across his face as his gaze intensified like a wolf narrowing in on prey.

Yasaman neared the doors, waiting for her stop to arrive. Her eyes darted towards the man, who had now gotten up at the same time and was waiting by the doors at the other end of the bus, his eyes unblinking and hungry. At her stop, she sped off the bus and began her trek home on the empty main road. The sound of a single pair of footsteps followed Yasaman, speeding up as she sped up. She cocked her head over her shoulder to find the man, breathing heavy with the same unbreakable gaze, trailing closely behind her.

Her eyes darted to the building as she began plotting her best route inside. She dreaded the entrance nearest to her, where the lights were dim and the door's lock always jammed. She knew it would slow her down enough for the man to close the gap. Instead, she zigzagged past the side door and onto a pathway towards the building's front entrance.

"Wait!" the man yelled at Yasaman. "Hang on!" Charging forward, she picked up her pace and yelled back, "GET THE FUCK AWAY FROM ME!" Yasaman's arms started to pump her forward as if at any moment they could catch the air and pull her into the sky. She looped into the parking lot and sprinted towards the building. Mom, who was where she always was, perched by the same window, caught a glance of Yasaman sprinting. Barefoot, she flung open the door and flew down six flights of stairs to get to the building entrance, where she reached out for Yasaman and pulled her in.

At the time, as I was watching TV on the couch, I had no idea how Mom had gone from peering out the window to launching herself downstairs. Though it wasn't the first time. Anything from a strange sound to an ambulance arriving would have Mom running downstairs to assess what had happened or offer support. I stood on top of the couch by the window, trying to see her. When Yasaman and Mom returned to the apartment, exasperated and barely speaking in full sentences, I was left with more questions than answers. Perhaps Mom was trying not to frighten me. I listened intently to their hushed conversation, trying to piece together bits and pieces of information—a man, the bus, running, gross, "the stupid side door never opens."

The more I witnessed these moments, the more aware I became that there were things "out there" to fear. Fear was more than what was etched into our imaginations, too; it was what was etched into our bodies. Fear had taken a chisel to the canvas of Yasaman's body, carving out a language of survival so different from mine, as it had to Mom's and Yara's. For Yasaman, it was a fuck-you carved into her face, shrinking men to mere nothings on the street. A mouth full of curse words. And legs that could run. And for Yara, her fixation on perfection, on fitting in. For Mom, her hawk-like self always perched somewhere, watching, ready to swoop down.

We were bonded by an unspoken understanding that we were to stick together and protect each other, fiercely. That was the system, that was the promise. What my armour would be was still unknown to me. For now, I watched the others, sheltered by their presence.

As Yasaman graduated and found work as an aesthetician at a mall north of the city, I felt the growing distance between her and us. She had met her boyfriend, Matt, at the mall; he was a light-eyed, shaved-head, scrawny white dude we knew little about. Or that's how Mom described him when Yasaman wasn't around. Worst of all, he was a high school dropout. For Mom, there was nothing worse than her kids ending up with a dropout. Mom had already married one, and the thought of her kids having a similar fate devastated her.

When Yasaman decided to leave home at twenty, all havoc broke loose as Mom tried to hold on to her.

"I'm moving out!" Yasaman yelled at Mom from her bedroom, packing her things.

"No, you're not," Mom screamed back, her feet stomping the floor.

"We have a plan. We're going to rent a basement."

"No, you're not. You're not moving in with that boy."

"Yes, I am! I'm moving out and I don't fucking care what you think."

"Yasaman—you're not moving out with him. I didn't move all this way for you to end up like me."

Mom's voice was now shrieking in the way she did when she was *really* upset. I stood near the end of the hallway, where I could hide behind the wall and still watch.

Mom stood in the doorway as Yasaman packed her clothes, blocking the way out with all her strength. "He's a loser. No education. No future. Nothing," she said firmly in English, staring directly into Yasaman's eyes. One after another, Yasaman hurled insults at Mom, and Mom hurled insults about Matt. When Yasaman was finished collecting all her belongings, she bodychecked Mom out of the doorway and into the wall. Mom tried to hold her back, grabbing at her clothes, but Yasaman was too strong for her.

With Yasaman's departure, Mom crumbled on the couch, sobbing. It had always been the four of us. None of us was ready for Yasaman to leave our wolf pack. Immediately, I felt more vulnerable and worried about whether we would be okay without each other. I sat next to Mom, my arms stretched around her, my body huddled into her corner of the couch. I had no armour, no way of protecting Mom from the pain and worry brought on by Yasaman's leaving. All I could offer was a softness that I sensed my mother needed. "You're a good mom," I reminded her. "It's going to be okay."

4

DAD

The common chorus that met anything that my father would say or do was a loud sigh. An *aughhhhhhh* let out by Yara, Yasaman or Mom on any given day. I could understand it. I loved him, but sometimes, his choices failed to make sense.

Every two weeks, when he'd returned from one of his trips, I hopped into the back seat of our blue van to pick him up with Mom, buzzing with the anticipation of seeing him again. I would climb up the stairs of his freight truck, and he'd pull me up onto the velvety seat. Our ritual was that I would take a lollipop from his collection next to his seat, and he would reach back and hand me a present from his travels. It was always something different. One time, a giant box of Pixy Stix from one of his skids. Another time, a plush toy from one of those claw machines they always have in roadside restaurants. His gifts were more than objects, they were tokens of love that I clung to while he was away.

Though our conversations were sparse, as a child, I felt immensely loved by my father. He was physically affectionate in a way that my mother and sisters weren't. His eyes would brighten at the sight of me and he'd lift me up and warmly pull me in against his soft body, the tightness of his hugs always bringing me a sense of soothing and ease. I followed him around the house like a puppy, wanting to show him anything new I had learned, or to list all of my latest accomplishments in school. He would praise everything I showed him, responding with "That's my girl," pulling at my cheeks. Rarely did he stay long. Two days, tops. And most of the time, he was driving around town, "sorting out his papers"—whatever that meant. I always yearned for more time with him.

Our first and only family trip was in the summer of 1999, when I was seven years old. It was rare for us to go anywhere. My father was always working and we were too broke to travel anyway. Though every year, Mom promised we'd go to Disneyland, and every year when I'd ask her when, she would respond with "*Inshallah*," which means "God willing." It took years for me to figure out that "Inshallah" sometimes meant "Sure, if some miracle were to fall upon us, then by the grace of God, yes."

My parents had decided we would go to Buffalo for discount clothing at an outlet mall. We drove two hours to the border—Mom with her bare feet up on the dashboard and a cup full of sunflower seeds in her hand; Yara, Yasaman and I in the back. Mom would crack the sunflower shells with her teeth and reach a handful of seeds back to me.

We finally approached the customs booths, where my father rolled down his window and leaned out with our passports. The border guard squinted down at the papers and looked back at us.

"Where are you headed?"

"Florida."

"How many days?"

"One."

"You're headed to Florida and you're coming back tomorrow?"

"Yes."

"You're going to Florida in one day?"

"Yes."

"Sir, please pull your car off to the side and come inside."

As soon as the window rolled up, everyone erupted with rage. No one understood why my father had said Florida. We had no plans to go to Florida. We had no plans to *say* we were going to Florida. It was comical if you were eight, and uncommitted to shopping in Buffalo.

"Why would you tell him we're going to Florida?"

"It was better."

"What do you mean? We're going to Buffalo. It's a one-day trip."

"Better to say Florida."

"Florida's a million years away, Dad."

"You should always say Florida."

Mom reluctantly sent Yara in with Dad. Even though Dad's job required him to deal with Americans regularly, Yara was still his appointed translator. At seventeen, she was used to it. We sat in the car for an hour, eating sunflower seeds and listening to Mom vent about how my father never thinks of anyone else. Eventually, an hour in, Yara emerged from the building and walked towards the car. Behind her, the border patrol agent came hammering through the doors, his face bright red.

"GET BACK INSIDE. WHEN I TELL YOU THAT YOU CAN LEAVE, YOU CAN LEAVE. DID I SAY YOU CAN LEAVE?"

Yara jumped and stiffened at the first sound of his voice, her whole body frozen for a moment. Frightened by his thundering voice, I froze, too. Yara then turned around, her eyes meeting his, and yelled at the top of her lungs: "I'M JUST TELLING MY MOM—"

Without letting her finish, he yelled back in his gruff voice: "GET BACK INSIDE. WE'RE NOT DONE." Sucking back tears, she marched back inside. My whole body was clenched as I waited for their return. I could understand that my father had done something wrong, but I couldn't make sense of why this man was yelling at my seventeen-year-old sister, who had no fault in all of this. I grew frustrated with my father, who was noticeably absent for all the yelling. It felt wrong to see her bear the consequences of his actions. Hours later, when the two of them were finally released from the interrogation room, Yara climbed into the car looking deflated, as did Dad. Our faces were collectively pale, as if we'd seen something terrible. We turned the car around and made our way home. Rarely had I been so disappointed in my father, who had soured our trip with an unnecessary lie.

For as long as I could remember, it felt like my parents were at odds with each other. It's hard to imagine a time when there was intimacy and romance between them. As I knew them, they were two ships passing in the night. Or worse, two ships colliding, threatening to sink each other. In my thirties, when I asked whether there were ever moments of intimacy between them, Mom talked about their travels together. Before any of us were born, barely able to afford their rent, Mom would join Dad on his long-haul travels in his truck, visiting far-off towns on the borders of Iran.

Their last solo journey together was in 1980, when they had travelled to Khuzestan, a province bordering Iraq. It was a popular place because of its port—fabrics and spices from all over the world would be brought over by ship and dispersed to various cities and towns in Iran via trucks. A couple hours into their time there, Mom noticed the unsettling arrival of tanks and soldiers in the distance, driving quickly towards them and swarming the city they were in. Everyone in the town was being told to gather their belongings and evacuate immediately. With urgency, the two of them hopped back into the freight truck and headed back to Esfahan. The next day, air strikes began, marking the beginning of the Iran–Iraq War.

As the war progressed, Esfahan had become a safer city compared to the towns on the border of Iran and Iraq. During that time, my mother had Yara, and twelve months later, Yasaman. It was hard for me to grasp how my family not only lived through a war, but managed to have children during it. I felt my mother trying to justify it, especially Yasaman's birth. She explained that it wasn't until a couple years in that Iraq began bombing near them. "It was so embarrassing," she shared, "being pregnant so quickly after birthing Yara." "Why?" I asked her, genuinely not understanding her embarrassment. "Because women are supposed to wait longer than that . . ." She trailed off.

When the bombs started landing in their city, their safety plan was to stay with Mom's younger sister, who lived on the edge of the city. She and her husband owned a large plot of land with a small house on it. Her eldest brother, Shahin, had set up a large tent outside and wired electric heating close to it so that they wouldn't freeze during the winter nights. The men slept outside in the tent; the women and children slept inside, in the one bedroom. The war had slowed down work, so they all spent their days together, waiting for the bombing to subside.

Mom recalled a particular night when my father insisted they gather their belongings and head back home. The two argued in front of everyone, my mother pleading that the bombs were continuing and that it'd be unsafe. It was a rare moment when others saw my father as my mother experienced him. Not the warm, charming man with a big smile plastered across his face, but rather, the stern patriarch who unilaterally made decisions and demanded they be followed. He doubled down, demanding she pack their things and get in the car. No explanation for his insistence, just a demand for them to return home immediately. Eventually, Mom surrendered and everyone got in the car.

It wasn't long before they started hearing the bombings again, closer and closer to their home. A few nights later, they were all jolted awake to the startling sound of the airport next to them being bombed. Yara was three years old, sobbing as her body shook uncontrollably. Mom lifted her into her arms, trying to comfort her, but nothing soothed her enough to stop the shaking. When the shaking stopped, Yara was left with a stutter. "Maman"—as my sisters called her in their early years—was now "ma-ma-ma-ma," and every time Mom heard her say her name, she felt the rush of guilt, of not having fought hard enough to keep her safe. It pained her to see how hard it was for Yara to utter words and how it seemed like she was always shaking now. The stutter dissappeared a year later, but Mom's distrust of my father remained. She knew that she couldn't lean on him; instead, she would need to protect her kids herself.

In the summer of 2002, when my father proposed taking me with him on one of his long-haul travels to Texas, Mom's objection was immediate. We all remembered when Yara went on a trip with him a few years before and came back a vegan. Yara had a deep love and respect for animals—all animals—so when my father proposed seeing a farm, I'm sure her response was a resounding yes. It was at that farm that she lovingly connected with the cows on the field before he took her to watch them be slaughtered. "And now she knows where meat comes from," my father responded to our confusion when they came back, finding the whole thing amusing.

On top of that, the declaration of the "war on terror," following the devastating events of 9/11 the previous year, had amplified Islamophobia, affirming a Western "us" and an Eastern "them." We had been inundated with images of brown-skinned, bearded men as the evil others, women in hijabs with their children living in poverty, needing to be liberated. The news channel was full of grieving Americans trying to make sense of the attacks, or speeches from President Bush and his administration, or images of al-Qaeda.

Admittedly, it wasn't the smartest time to go, but my father was convinced it was a chance for me to see a little of the world, and I wanted to spend time with my dad, who I missed. So my mother reluctantly agreed.

We drove towards the American border in the thick July heat, passing by long stretches of farmlands, southern crops and slow cattle. At the border, we were slotted in a line that required a search of the truck. "Why don't we get to go through?" I gestured at the trucks moving straight ahead to the border, quickly passing through. Instead of answering, my father pulled into the lineup and reached for his papers, trying to make sure everything was in order. I looked into the side mirror, noticing the long lineup of sweaty brown men waiting their turn, some with long beards, some with hair wrapped, some with bushy eyebrows and some with big, thick glasses. Some were Muslim, some were Sikh.

It was obvious to me that we were being lumped in together because of our brown skin. All this time, I had watched news coverage of 9/11 and the war on terror, and it had not occurred to me that *we* would be perceived as threats. At that age, I had categorized us as a different kind of "brown." The Westernized kind, who not only empathized with the grief of Americans, but shared in their feelings of vulnerability and their fears of being attacked. I was only beginning to feel the hostility towards us, the suspicion that we were dangerous.

After hours in line, our turn arrived and we drove up to the white border agent hastily waving us forward.

The agent approached my father's window with his eyebrows arched and a piercing gaze, mumbling something that even I couldn't understand. "What?" Dad responded. The officer's brows furrowed even more—"TURN OFF YOUR ENGINE. TURN. OFF. YOUR. ENGINE!" Startled, Dad smiled uncomfortably and promptly turned off his engine. The officer then mumbled another question, his cap covering his face as he looked down at his clipboard. Dad responded again: "What?" The officer chuckled, looked out to the line behind him and returned with his piercing gaze: "Are you stupid? Are you fucking stupid? I'm asking you to . . ."

Dad's voice quieted, his hands quivering as he reached for documents and log books tucked into the folder on his right. Sitting in the passenger seat, feet barely touching the ground, I disappeared into visions of the border agent choking on his gum. The gum he chewed so loudly as he called my dad stupid. I could feel the rage bubbling inside. I wanted him to feel small, too. Like an insignificant pebble.

"And who are you?" the border agent snapped at me, thrusting me back into reality. My words caught in my mouth. "That's my daughter," Dad responded with an appeasing smile.

"No, I don't need to hear it from you. I need to hear it from her," the agent said. Just as Dad had done, I softened. Curled my lips into a stiff smile, as best I could, and said: "I'm his daughter." "This man is your father?" he asked again. "Yes," I responded. He stared at me a while longer, as if to pause for a change in my answer. Eventually, he waved us off and we continued on our way.

"Why was he like that?" I asked Dad, feeling pity for him. Without looking at me, he responded, "They are stupid." Taking his cue for silence, I ruminated quietly on the humiliation ritual we had just endured to be granted entrance into the country. I missed my mother, who would be livid right now, venting about the Americans, cursing them for their hostility and their audacity to even suggest that I wasn't their child. With my mother, there would have been someone to reflect the same injustice I felt about the experience. Instead, I had my father, whose silence left me feeling alone in the whole thing.

I retreated into fantasies of what I might have said, had I been armoured the way my sisters were. Sharp-tongued and brave enough to stand up for myself, instead of smiling politely. I knew, even then, that nothing good would've come from it, but perhaps the mere fantasy of it helped to ease my feelings of vulnerability.

Dad played Hayedeh cassettes most of the time during our trip. It sounded like ancient, old-people Iranian music from the early 1900s. I would half read through a pile of books I had borrowed from the library, my feet folded on the passenger seat, occasionally gazing at the trees and the quiet, featureless landscape. From time to time, you would hear the static fuzziness of the CB radio, followed by the coarse sound of men talking.

Usually, it was about the highway. Where police officers were stopped. Where the accidents were. Boring stuff that I could tune out easily. Sometimes, it sounded like a private conversation I was overhearing. I remember one conversation between two men that made me want to crawl out of my skin.

"Yeah, she had some big tits on her there," one voice giddily said.

"Yeah, some are them are sexy, some of them ain't," another laughed.

I turned to my father, who drove in silence, his eyes fixed on the road. I asked him what the conversations on the CB radio were about, gesturing innocently to the radio. It felt like watching a movie with your parents and having a sex scene show up onscreen. Gross, and incredibly uncomfortable.

"Radio. We talk about what's happening, where the police are, what roads are blocked," he mechanically explained, no acknowledgement of what we were hearing in that moment.

Slowly, the distance between us was growing. His eyes refocused on the road and we kept driving. Still uncomfortable, I looked back down to my book, and tried to block out the voices.

There were few things I loved more than a truck stop diner. The tantalizing array of hot, greasy foods—mashed potatoes and gravy, saucy steaks, crispy chicken. We parked at the chain truck stop and I slowly climbed down the steps of the freight truck with my clothes, my bag of shower supplies and my towel clutched in my arms, Dad waiting at the bottom to help me down.

I followed him into the storefront, to an old white man sitting at the cash register. "Hello!" my father said, exaggerating his enunciation of the word (an exclamation mark often ended his hellos on this side of the border). "What do ya need," the man asked flatly." "I need . . . eh . . . two shower," my father responded.

We walked into the dimly lit diner with leather-seated booths and round-bodied white men chuckling with waitresses. When our waitress came by, Dad amped up his cheerfulness. He Americanized his accent as best he could, and spoke loudly.

"Would you like to hear today's special?" she asked.

"Special, as in free?" he chuckled.

The waitress didn't laugh back. This was a version of my father I hadn't seen before. One where his usual warmth and charm fell flat amongst Americans who continued to dismiss and reject him. With every interaction, there was a sadness that quietly chirped in me. The charm I saw in my father didn't translate here, where there was often an undertone of hostility and suspicion.

When my mountain of mashed potatoes and gravy arrived, he commented on how grand the food in America was, and how it always came in truckloads. I tried to meet him in his cheerfulness, aware of how humiliating it must have felt to be treated with so little respect.

As he paid for the food, I wandered over to a wooden board plastered with the faces of women and girls from as far back as the eighties. Mostly black-and-white images. As many as thirty or forty, with "MISSING" boldly labelled at the top. I hadn't seen many women at the truck stops—definitely none as drivers. Only a few women here and there in washrooms. In retrospect, some of those had likely been hitchhikers and sex workers—but they'd made the washrooms a little less quiet and daunting. This board featured the most women I had seen. I suddenly felt vulnerable, fearful that I would go missing like one of the girls on the board.

Not sensing my worry, Dad guided me to the women's shower area and gestured at the door. "Listen, don't talk to anyone. Don't go with anyone. Once you're done, you wait for me here. If I'm not here, you go back in the women's area and wait," he instructed me quickly before disappearing into the men's shower.

I entered into the women's showers with goosebumps up my neck, and my heart beating double its regular speed. It was empty and quiet enough that I could hear single drops of water from the shower heads. I wondered if women and girls had gone missing here in these showers.

I nearly ripped through my clothes from pulling them off so quickly. I made a plan: Be fast, but also, be quiet. I wore my shower sandals and stood under the water, peering out every few seconds through the curtain to make sure I was still alone. When I was done, I grabbed my towel, stepped out of the showers and heard a squeaking that made my body jolt. I sighed deeply, realizing it was just the sound of my own sandals. The coast was still clear. I dressed quickly, pulling my clothes over my damp skin.

"Roza," I heard Dad calling from the other side of the wall. I rushed out to him, my clothes half thrown in the bag I had brought. "You didn't brush your hair? You have a comb," Dad complained, clearly frustrated. "And you didn't even dry yourself properly?" he continued as we walked back to his truck.

When we got back, my father pulled out his comb and started brushing my hair. And even as I protested, he continued. *Mom would never make me brush out my curls*, I thought. "You have to look proper. In this world, you have to look proper," he kept repeating. I stopped resisting, feeling the pain of each stroke as the comb tugged through my knots.

He had always had a particular fixation on how he looked, spending ample time in the washroom grooming himself. I would notice his morning routines, where he would wet his hair and comb through it again and again. Then he would wash his face gently, towel it off and dab cologne on his neck. It was like he entered a meditative state each time, his face relaxed and his spirit calm. I wonder now what this fixation was about. And whether it was about his own sense of respectability and dignity in a world that so often diminished him. The sense that if he could only present as respectable, he would *be* respectable.

On the way back to Canada, my father lost my passport, which was *very* unfortunate timing. While he seemed calm and relaxed, I felt petrified that I would never get home. Where would they send me? Was I Iranian? They certainly wouldn't let me stay here, in the US—would they? Would I see my mom again? Dad continued driving towards the border and offering short replies like "It's going to be fine" and "Don't worry." His phone kept ringing because Mom kept calling us, equally terrified that I wouldn't be let back in the country. From my seat, I could hear her yelling at my dad, saying "Typical you, not thinking of your kids, not thinking of anyone but yourself."

I was flooded with the memory of being stranded at the border for hours when Dad decided to say "Florida" instead of "Buffalo." On top of my regular anxiety about my lost passport was a secondary worry about what would come out of his mouth. Internally, I prayed that he would at least tell the truth and explain that he lost the passport.

With my new realization that Dad wasn't someone I could rely on, my fears intensified. I started brushing my hair as we approached the border. Pulled the curls down with my fingers as if that would straighten them out. Perhaps there *was* something to looking proper, I thought. It didn't help. Instead, the disgruntled border security officer sent us inside to a tiny office where another stern-looking border agent interrogated me. I sat upright, smiled politely and crossed my hands on top of each other, hoping to appear likeable, compliant and trustworthy. The interview took a strange turn when I realized that most concerning to them was not whether I was actually a citizen of Canada, but rather, whether my father was my *actual* father.

"Is this man your father?"

"Yes."

"Has this man stolen you from your family?"

"No."

"Are you sure this man is your father?"

"Yes."

"Who are your parents?"

"This is my dad, my mom is at home."

"Why is your mom home?"

"She works."

Having to prove that my father was my actual father was something I wasn't prepared for. After I repeated again and again that my father was, in fact, my father, they eventually allowed us to return to the truck and cross over to Canada. I walked back to the truck feeling more like an adult than an a ten-year-old kid. It was ironic—to spend so much time convincing them that he was my Dad, at a time when I felt such distance and confusion about who he actually was. We were no closer now, no more known to each other after having travelled together, than before. Instead, the distance between us was increasing, igniting a disillusionment that would continue to unravel my relationship with him. Where I once missed and yearned for him, I now desperately longed to be back home with my mother and sisters.

5

HOME

When I touched the leathery cover of my Iranian passport for the first time at seven years old, I felt claimed. Despite what my sisters had been saying about me being Canadian, it never quite fit for me. I wanted to belong to Iran. My sisters' birth was proof of their Iranian-hood. But this little booklet was mine.

It was 1999 and Khaleh (Aunt) Sima, Mom's best friend in Toronto, was the first to see our passports up close. Khaleh Sima was one of those big-spirited aunties you always looked forward to seeing. Chocolates and pastries in one hand, gossip in the other. Fair, freckled skin, pin-straight short auburn hair and a joyfully round body that she dressed exclusively in bold patterns. Sometimes, she would get so passionate that her low-and-slow Farsi turned into a high-boil Turkish rant, hands waving emphatically in the air. Neither I nor my mother understood Turkish, but we nodded along, somehow comprehending what it all meant. I felt struck by how Khaleh Sima's borderless tongue seemed to flow effortlessly between lands and peoples.

Soon after Khaleh arrived at our apartment, Mom emerged from the kitchen with a silver tray of hot chai and sugar cubes. The coffee table was crowded with enough food for five—a bowl of mixed fruit piled high, a bowl of pistachios, a bowl of sunflower seeds, a plate of baklava and a box of assorted pastries.

Gently, she handed her friend our passports. "How many years has it been since you went home?" Khaleh asked, flipping through the pages and finally landing on our photos. "Ten," Mom said with a familiar whale of a sigh. The kind she gave when she finished a phone call with one of her sisters, or her Baba. "We were too scared to go back before now. God knows what could have happened . . ." Her voice trailed off. "Still we don't know—will they let us return? You know how they are." She scowled. The fact that we were all citizens now didn't seem to matter to Mom. She still feared the cruel hand of the regime, keeping her captive. Like the airport officials would suddenly tear up her passport and refuse to let her leave. Anxiously, she massaged her hands.

"Maryam?" Khaleh asked aloud, pointing to the words beside my face.

"They wouldn't let me use Roza. They say it's not Iranian, it's not Muslim, so they rejected it," Mom explained, shaking her head.

"Ridiculous, for real, it's ridiculous," Khaleh responded, both of them now shaking their heads.

"Maryam is the name of my great-grandmother, though, and I've always loved it." Mom smiled.

I sat on the side of the couch closest to the window, far enough to feel invisible, near enough to hear the conversation between them, quietly biting into baklava. My ears perked up when I heard the name *Maryam*. I wondered, if not from Iran, if not from Islam, where did *Roza* come from? (Years later, I would learn that it came from one of the soap operas my mother watched obsessively during her first year in Canada.) *Roza* always felt too ambiguous for a brown-skinned girl like me.

I yearned for one of those ethnically specific names that read like a map home. A traditionally Iranian name, like Azadeh or Leila. They had roots, and history, and identity. Instead, I had Roza—and a pattern of saying, "No, I'm not that—I'm this."

"No, I'm not Mexican—I'm Iranian."

"No, I'm not Indian—I'm Iranian."

"No, I'm not mixed—I'm just Iranian."

Not that, this.

I asked my mother if I could see the passport, and she begrudgingly allowed me to hold it. I flipped through the pages carefully until I arrived at a small photo of me staring at the camera with flat affect, pale skin and hair covered under a hijab. She looked like a Maryam, I thought.

During the winter of 2001, there was just enough money to send Mom and me to Iran, marking my first visit home. Since we had so few photos of Iran, most of what I colourfully imagined about the Middle East was a complicated mixture of the Persian TV show we watched on Saturday mornings, images of war in Afghanistan after 9/11, and Disney's *Aladdin*.

The moment the plane hit the tarmac in Tehran, I started crying. When Mom asked what was happening, I had no way of explaining it to myself, let alone her. After over fifteen hours of travel, my body felt foreign to me. It did as it wanted— nausea, fainting, tears. She wiped my tears with her thumbs, tightened a black hijab around my face, and took a deep breath as we stood up to gather our belongings. Nervousness gnawed my belly as we waited to disembark. Perhaps it was both my own uncertainty of what was to come and that of my mother, who was massaging her hands with a familiarly pensive expression on her face.

She broke into a smile, though, as we caught a glimpse of the arrivals section, crowded with over fifty people holding balloons and flowers. The glass wall between those entering and those waiting for loved ones could barely contain them. It suddenly became clear that the people banging their hands against the glass were yelling our names. "That's our family," Mom whispered to me. Mom, overcome with tears, clutched my hand and moved us into the chaotic embrace of the crowd.

Passed from one person to another, each kissing my face and hugging me tightly, I started crying uncontrollably again. This time, overwhelmed by it all and wishing I could crawl under the chairs and hide. I knew these were family members, yet they all felt like strangers. Each time I was pulled to another, my chest constricted more, making it harder and harder to breathe. Eventually I surrendered to the chaos, allowing myself to be pulled from one person to another like I was floating in the ocean, at the whim of the tide and waves.

Outside the airport, I grabbed Mom's hand tightly again, grasping for ease and soothing. We piled into a car that looked like something out of the seventies. Six of us squeezed into the back, two in the front. When the others tried to pull me onto their laps, I clung to Mom, smiling shyly.

Music blasted from the speakers, people honked with excitement. I watched cars speeding across lanes, motorcycles weaving in and out of traffic, and quickly realized that no one seemed to care about driving rules here. As we twisted and turned through narrow side streets, I closed my eyes and smelled the air, thick with a mixture of gasoline, cologne and freshly cut trees. I kept my eyes closed, feeling more at ease that way.

Ten cars lined up outside my grandparents' small yellow-brick bungalow home, everyone honking and yelling like drunk fans after a soccer victory. Baba Ali, my grandfather, stood outside the house, grinning from ear to ear. A medium-build man with grey hair and brown skin spotted with age, wearing a handsome grey suit and white dress shirt. Mom opened the car door and flung herself into his arms, gripping him tightly. Her tears stained his suit, his tears stained her hijab. We all stood still around them, watching them in silence. A sight that felt so sorrowful, a sharp contrast to the joyful ride here.

Up until then, it hadn't occurred to me that my mother was someone's baby. That she had a father, and a mother, and sisters, and brothers, and a whole community that missed her deeply here, ached for her, counted the days until her return. Her body trembled as she let out waves of big sobs, Baba Ali continuing to hold her. I tried to suck back my tears, overcome with the sadness of seeing my mother in this distraught state—so small, childlike and fragile.

When their bodies untwined from the hug, Mom fell silent. She opened and closed her mouth, but there came no words, no utterances. She tried again and again, but she couldn't make a single sound. Later, she would say that she'd felt like something had caught in her throat, blocking words from moving up and out.

As the night progressed, her eyes puffed up like she had been sobbing for days. Her skin paler than usual, her voice still gone. I stayed close to her, one hand always attached to the hijab that hung around her neck like a scarf. No matter how tightly I clung to her, I still felt alone. Selfishly, I wondered if I would have to navigate this new place solo now, unable to lean on Mom like I had always done.

Inside the house I looked around, noticing the absence of any chairs or tables. Instead, there were rugs and pillows all around and people sitting in every corner. My grandmother, my aunties and cousins took turns cozying up next to me. "*Moosh bokhoratet*," my grandmother would say to me, a term of endearment meaning "May a mouse eat you." Others squeezed my cheeks and said, "*Ghorboonet beram, azizam*," roughly meaning "May I sacrifice myself for you, my love." Mostly, I smiled and sat quietly next to them, as if I, too, had lost my voice. Even that was endearing to them. In part my silence was because I had grossly overestimated my comprehension skills, now realizing that without Mom's help, my Farsi skills were below average.

Late into the night, each of my cousins helped lay blankets and pillows on the ground, eventually covering the entire floor. All the women stayed over, rallying around Mom in hopes of bringing her voice back. I lay next to my mother that night—Mom on one side, a wall on the other. Turned my back to hers and held my hand over my mouth as I cried. Perhaps I was in some form of shock, feeling the dissonance between what I had imagined and what actually happened. I had imagined that my connection to my family would be instantaneous. That they would feel like one big hug, warming up my soul. And in some ways, they did feel like one big hug—but instead of warming up my soul, it felt overpowering. The more they wanted to be near me, the more suffocated I felt. All I wanted was to return home, to Canada.

Over the next two days, my grandmother and aunties tried everything to help Mom find her voice again. They went to the doctor and he confirmed there were no medical issues; more likely it was just a shock response. They tried herbal mixtures, and teas, and fresh fruits, and fresh air. They tried warm compresses and cold compresses. They tried holding her in their arms and rocking her gently.

On the third day, the colour started coming back into her cheeks, her eyes no longer puffy. And on that day, as one of her sisters handed her her afternoon chai, she finally spoke: "Thank you, sister." They all cheered and hugged my mother, welcoming her back.

We woke to Baba Ali's morning *dua*. He prayed so loud, the running joke amongst my aunties was that he was trying to make sure Allah could hear him from down here. "Baba is still cool." Mom laughed with her siblings as they all watched him in awe, hopping onto his motorbike in the mid-morning. Off to buy some fresh bread and herbs. It was as if my aunties were still kids, seeing their young father off from the window, hands pressed against the glass.

During the seventies and eighties, Baba Ali had owned a dry cleaning shop around the corner, where he'd spent most of his days. Always sharply dressed, his shirts perfectly ironed, his suits tailored to his body. Mom described him as a charming man who surrounded himself often with beloved friends, believing community was more important than capitalism.

It was hard for me to reconcile Mom's version of her father with the man I was witnessing now. He was in his seventies, and sure, still riding a motorbike across the city. But now, excepting the volume of his prayers, he was more reserved. A quiet man who spent most of his time cleaning herbs, listening to his radio, praying or running errands.

Though our exchanges were mostly through warm smiles, I was drawn to him for who my mother became in his presence. Observing from inside the house through the floor-to-ceiling glass windows facing the front yard, I watched as Mom unravelled a picnic blanket and spread it on the ground. Baba Ali carried his tiny radio with him outside, turned up the volume and took a seat next to her.

He emptied one bag of herbs, seemingly parsley, onto the blanket. Baba showed Mom how to pick apart the parsley cloves from the stems—cloves into a container, stems into a bag. She watched his hands first and followed after. There was something soothing about seeing my mother following, not leading as she always did back home. Not her usual hawk self, perched up above somewhere, watching intently. She was softer here—slower and lighter in ways that I had only caught glimpses of in our kitchen, when she was cooking.

In the mornings, my grandmother, Khanoom, would be preparing breakfast for us in a kitchen so small, it fit three people, tops. Feta on one plate, along with a plate of herbs and pita bread. Butter with different kinds of jam and warm *noon barbari*, a type of flatbread. Tea, along with sugar cubes for *chai shireen*, meaning "sweet tea"—a common breakfast addition. My aunties would lay the spread of food on the ground and I would follow them, waiting for them to give me tasks—like placing the utensils out by the plates, or bringing the water jug out.

I started sitting between my grandmother and my mother during breakfast. My grandmother would lovingly gaze into my eyes, grab my hand and say, "*Nooshi joon,*" a common phrase around food, meaning "May your soul be nourished." I smiled back, growing more comfortable in her warm presence. Her scent now a familiar one that I enjoyed taking in, trying to place what it was. She pulled some pita and feta onto my plate, along with a handful of herbs. Her hands shook as she placed the plate back in front of me, a shaking that never seemed to stop, even when she held my hand. "Look at how good she eats," she said, smiling at my mother, who nodded, affirming my appetite, too. "She's always been this way. She eats like us." They laughed. When everyone finished their plates, I started putting things back in the kitchen, following my aunties. "Look at what a girl she is, what a lady," my grandmother said, my aunties affirming the sentiment. I could do no wrong here. Any move I made was met with a narrative celebrating how good I was.

Most exciting were the days when Amou Javid, my father's brother, came to visit. His eyes reminded me of my father's, and his jokes were equally corny. Finding parts of myself in his face was easy to do, given that he looked exactly like my dad. But while my father was a round-bodied man, often compared to Santa Claus, Amou Javid was a very, very thin man. His hugs felt bony, unlike my father's soft bear hugs.

Though my mother had a tumultuous relationship with my father's family, Amou Javid was an exception. "Javid is a good man. It's too bad they never married him off," Mom reminisced to my aunties, who all agreed.

Every few days, Amou Javid would buzz into my grandparents' house, always with something different in hand. Some days, it was flowers. Other days, it was pastries. It became our regular midday event. "Come sit, kid. Unless you have somewhere to be?" He would laugh, knowing full well I had nowhere to be. I loved his laugh. Short, staccato chuckles that shook his entire body. *Ha, ha, ha, ha.* His eyes disappeared when he laughed, just like mine. A deck of cards in hand, he would shuffle and announce the newest game he was going to teach me. Last time, it was Hokm. This time, it was a variation of Crazy Eights. He taught me not only how to play cards, but also how to cheat when playing cards, which felt equally important.

Take an extra card off the top, but don't let anyone see you. Drop two crap cards down "by accident" and pick up two good ones. Keep picking up two until you get the good ones. Look at the next card when you try to pick up your cards, so you know what other players have. Peek at the cards of others discreetly when they go to pick up a new card—that's when they're least suspecting. If you have too many cards in the end, drop the one you don't want under your legs.

No one had ever sat me down like this, assumed the role of teacher, guided me with such joy and patience. Is that what uncles and aunties do? Back home, I learned on my own. If Yara or Yasaman taught me anything, it was always with a teenager's undertone of annoyance and impatience.

Some days, my cousin Amin would join us outside, playing cards. "Oh god, you're here again," my grandmother would joke. "He's going to eat all of our plums," Baba Ali would yell, also teasing. Amin and I were the closest in age, so naturally, he came around often.

Amou Javid had me shuffle the cards, tipping his head and winking as if to say, *Remember what I taught you*. I would try to remember all the tips and tricks. After a few wins, Amin threw down his cards and said, "I knew it! You're cheating! I saw you." "No, I'm not!" I would respond, defensively. Amou Javid and I would look at each other, eyes sparkling, both knowing the truth we'd hold between us in secrecy.

It took less than two weeks to feel at home in Esfahan, enamoured of the people and places alike. Home was an overflowing thing here. Doors were always open, people always shuffling in and out. Swaths of family members showed up every day, throughout the day. Some would funnel in for midday siesta breaks, which I had grown fond of. Some would show up for dinner after work, offering to support my grandmother in the kitchen.

I grew to find comfort in the seemingly over-the-top intimacy of family here. I was never alone. Out and about, my cousins would make a point to introduce me to their friends as the "*khareji* cousin," meaning "foreigner," which felt special. They would have me tag along to their volleyball games, their salon appointments, their park visits. They would negotiate who got me, and on which days and nights.

My aunties and cousins cuddled up to me, inspecting my face, looking for all the parts resembling them. "She has Baba

Ali's nose," Khaleh Zare remarked. "You should show her pictures of her other grandmother," Khanoom said, referring to my father's mother, who had passed away before my birth. "Her eyes and eyebrows are her," Khaleh Soraya chimed in. I inspected their faces, too. Charmed by any proof in their faces that I was one of them. A similar musicality in my voice existed, a distinct local way of bending and shortening and stretching words. Even I was amused by how much this place, these people, lived inside me.

Over time, I tried to take in as much of the culture as I could—the politeness, the sweetness, the warmth, even the ways they would gently make fun of each other. "Hide the plums!" I would yell, the room erupting in laughter, as Amin entered the house. I was taking mental field notes of things I wanted to integrate into myself. Some were reminders of things I already knew, like the practice of *tarof*; the ritual was to say no to any offering a minimum of three times, out of politeness. It always felt playful and warm. Then there were the things that felt newer. I was amused by how I would compliment my cousins' jewellery and they would literally take it off their body and hand it to me. To which I would, of course, engage in tarof and say no, refusing to accept it. Or how guests visiting my grandparents' house, pastries in hand, would often say, "I'm sorry I didn't bring more." Until now, "thank you" had always been a simple utterance of "*merci*," but now I wanted to say "*dased dard nakooneh*" like they did, which roughly translated to "I hope your hands don't hurt." Or my favourite: if you sat with your back to someone, you apologized, to which they would respond, "A flower has no front or back."

Sweet and tart, the culture felt akin to a pomegranate. Each seed a new cultural teaching I wanted to consume and embody.

After playing cards, Amin and I decided we would play soccer in the alleyway in front of the house. We cracked open the heavy gate and started passing the ball back and forth. Suddenly, a woman in a long chador started yelling. At first, I didn't realize she was yelling at me, a nine-year-old kid. The more I looked around, trying to see who she was yelling at, the closer she came, until her finger was wagging towards me. Her words became clearer. She was admonishing me for being in public without a hijab. With my heart racing and stomach turning, I rushed back to my grandparents' house, telling my aunties what had happened. "Oh, don't mind them," my aunties yelled, laughing about the whole incident. I stood there, frightened, confused and, above all, ashamed. For what? For doing something seemingly wrong, and not knowing exactly what that was. I asked my mother if it was true—that I'd done something wrong by being outside with my hair visible. Mom explained that the laws were different here—I was old enough to wear a hijab, and required to do so by law. "But don't worry about it—the older generation are more uptight about it," she responded, as if it was no big thing.

I was too young then to understand how the current regime had appropriated the hijab as a tool of oppression against women. The hijab itself wasn't oppressive, as the narratives around 9/11 seemed to push in the news; the patriarchal systems that seized on it as a mechanism of control were. Amongst our community in Toronto, the hijab had felt relatively neutral. I had understood it as a personal choice once one was old enough to contemplate their own practice of modesty. Here, it wasn't a conversation with oneself nor a choice; it was a demand.

At that time, my frustration lay in not understanding how the rules of modesty applied to me, a child. Or how a fully grown woman could be so angered by me, a child, not wearing a hijab. Of course, with no one fully explaining it to me and the others wanting me to brush it off, I worried about it for the rest of the trip. I wore my hijab tightly, even trying on my grandmother's chador, which she and my aunts found both endearing and comedic—a chador being a body-length cloak that covered one's hair and extended to just above one's feet. I was serious about wearing a chador out in public, as ridiculous as it looked on me, dragging across the floor. The others, sensing my anxieties, assured me a hijab was sufficient as they pulled it off me.

"Take your clothes off," Mom told me, standing in the bathroom with my auntie and grandmother crammed in. "Why?" I asked. "We're going to scrub you," she responded, as if that was an everyday thing we did. By then, I had become more comfortable with my grandmother and aunties. Even so, the thought of getting naked in front of them was awkward and unsettling. I stripped down to my underwear and stood there in the shower, waiting. Khaleh Soraya put one hand into a scrubbing mitt and held a round white object in the other. She smiled reassuringly, telling me that I was going to feel much better when they were done. I believed her.

Sefid-ab, Khaleh explained, was an ancient scrub used to purify the body of dead skin. Khaleh moved my hair to the side and started scraping my back. The rough texture peeled dirt off my body, browning the water around my feet. When she was done, Mom undressed and took a turn in the shower. Khaleh started scraping her body, too.

"Do you remember how much our grandmother used to do this for us?" Khaleh said.

"And brush our hair. Remember? With olive oil," Mom responded.

For the rest of the time, the scrubbing happened in silence, just the sound of the hard sefid-ab scraping against her skin, peeling off layers of dirt. No comments about my body—my pudgy stomach, the growing hair on my arms. I had aunties back in Toronto who felt like community to me, but I had never felt closeness like this. The ease I eventually felt in having my body scrubbed in this way quieted my discomfort at being naked. Instead, I felt deeply loved and cared for.

The relationship my mother had with her sister was profoundly intimate in ways I had never experienced with my own sisters. The most intimate memory I had with Yara was a single moment years before when we'd swung on a swing together, me sitting on her lap, facing her. I remember wanting to tuck in and hug her, and refraining, knowing the unabashed rejection I would swiftly face. With Yasaman, there were no moments of closeness I could recall—though there were pictures of her holding me as a toddler, convincing me that there was once a time when she held affection for me.

There my mother stood in that shower, wearing only her underwear, seemingly wholly comfortable. Her face soft and easeful as her sister scrubbed her shoulders and her arms. To love and care for each other so openly, so vulnerably, so abundantly, felt commonplace here. I felt a growing deep reverence for the closeness my mother and her sisters had.

We might as well have been dressed in black, wrapped in chadors and headed to a funeral. We dragged our feet all the way to the home of Amou Reza, my father's eldest brother. It was my first time meeting the rest of my father's family, aside from my beloved Amou Javid, and it was obvious from my mother's grim expression that the visit was one of duty, not desire.

It was a murky thing, Mom's relationship with my father's family. They were cruel, unkind and weird, she would often tell me. A sentiment echoed by my sisters. Yasaman recalled, at eight years old, asking for a glass of water, to which my father's father walked over and poured an entire pitcher over her head. His hyena laugh echoed through the home and sometimes, still, her ears. A cruel joke no one understood. It was what would become my sisters' last memory of him, which perhaps explains why no one in my family cried when he passed away—not even my father.

We arrived just in time for dinner, a carefully thought-out decision by my mother, who had prepared for limited conversation and a swift exit. Amou Reza's family stood waiting at the door, nervous smiles stretched across their faces. They reached in for hugs and kisses, to which I uneasily obliged.

The home was traditional. If there was a standard test for Iranian homes, this would be it: a series of Persian rugs, china displayed behind a glass cabinet, and a coffee table set with nuts, fruit and sweets. Amou Reza was a tall, slender man with an unsettling demeanour. He spoke as if he always had more to say—every pause and period an ellipsis, as if he was about to name something everyone was trying to forget. He called my mother by her first name, Mina—which felt bold for someone she rarely spoke of, or to.

When he smiled, his eyes thinned into quarter moons and I saw my father. I saw the same side-parted hair, the same creases around his eyes, the same brown freckles on his face. I tried not to stare too much, or to see my father or myself in him. *I'm not supposed to like him*, I told myself.

His wife, Zan-amou Roya, brought out a tray full of steeped black tea and sugar cubes. My mother leaned forward to take one glass for herself with two sugar cubes, and one glass for me, and thanked her politely. She placed one cube between her teeth and sipped the tea through it while gazing at the glass, gliding her fingers along its simple pattern. Her eyes soft but intent, as if looking for something specific. She put down the glass abruptly, still with soft eyes and a pleasant smile.

Soon after, they set the *sofreh* on the ground, dishes lying from one side of the living room to the other. There were bright orange stews, saffron-infused rice and fresh *noon barbari*. I was eyeing the beloved tahdig that sits in the centre of the sofreh, the crown jewel of any Iranian meal, but my mother's gaze became fixated on the plates. Her brows momentarily furrowed in what I thought was curiosity. She was both here— looking at the plates—and somewhere else. For the rest of the meal, I wondered where she had gone. When we were done, we stayed for a brief conversation about what it felt like to return to Iran after so long. My mother noted apologetically that we had to return home to my grandmother's house and rushed us out the door.

"Don't be strangers," Zan-amou Roya smiled. "Our home is your home."

During the taxi ride home, Mom looked like a balloon with so much air pumped into it, one poke and she'd go *pop*. I knew not to say anything. When we finally got to my grandmother's house, she erupted in equal parts rage and sadness. My grandmother and Khaleh Soraya pulling her in closer, hugging her as tears poured out.

"*Thoseweremine*. Those were mine. The plates, the tea glasses, the china—they were all mine," she said to my grandmother, who looked at her as if understanding exactly what she was referencing. Mom's eyes flooded by memories she had long exiled. Her voice barely scratching the surface of the loss.

I didn't yet understand the magnitude of my mother's loss, or the story she was alluding to. I could sense that the loss and betrayal she was feeling were about more than the dishes. In between cries, I heard her talking about their journey to Canada. Whispers from my aunt, saying, "Don't you remember when you returned here? You know, we still never told anyone when you came back." I wondered if there was more to the story about how my parents came to Canada than what they'd shared. The story had always been that they came to Canada to give us, their kids, a better life. It was a happy story, one of hope, and joy, and optimism. In that brief moment, it wasn't light that shined through the cracks in Mom's story—it was a thundering sadness.

I lay awake that night, wondering what I was missing.

On our last day, everyone sobbed so much, you would think someone had died. At my grandparents' house, in the car, in the airport, as we walked through security. "It's okay, we'll come back again," my mother said, trying to console me, and perhaps herself, too. "When?" I mumbled back through my sobs, mucus dripping from my nose. I wanted to grip this place with both my hands and refuse to leave.

It had been easier before I felt the soft embrace of my aunties and cousins, or knew how to cheat at cards with Amou Javid. To know this magnitude of love was a double-edged sword. To have loved and been loved so abundantly, so intimately—and to have to leave it behind, with no plan for return. Would it be another decade before I felt their embrace? Would it be two? This place had changed me. Where there was love, there was now an accompanying ache—a deep yearning and longing to be with them.

As we waited for our plane home on the other side of the airport, I curled into Mom's body. "Why did you have to leave this place?" I asked my mother between sobs, as if bartering and begging to stay. "Why?" I asked again. She looked away, pulling my body closer into hers.

This time, we both knew exactly why we were crying.

6

BOY

To mark the end of elementary school, Priya and I decided to perform a soulful slow dance, choreographed to Justin Timberlake's "Cry Me a River." I had known Priya since grade three, only becoming closer friends with her that year. Priya was Tamil, like many of those living in our community. Brown-skinned with big brown eyes that looked naturally lined, a bindi on her forehead that I admired and, almost always, a big, bright smile. Her mother reminded me of my own, warmly inviting me into their home and offering food and water before I could even slip off my shoes. Her home smelled no different than the hallways of our apartment building. I took a whiff of the incense that filled her living room while admiring the Hindu statues and images scattered around.

We sat on the floor of a slightly empty room, both eagerly landing on the Justin Timberlake tune. Both of us familiar with it because of how often it played on radio stations. Buzzing with excitement, I imagined re-enacting its story of betrayal and heartache. There was a certain expertise I had acquired by that time. Though I had no relationship experience, I *did* have two summers spent reading the steamy romances I'd secretly picked up at garage sales with my parents. My parents rarely, if ever, zoomed in to the details of what I was reading. Instead, they gazed at me with glowing pride, thrilled to see me choose a book each time. My avid reading a sign that they had raised me right.

For a few weeks, Priya and I practised the choreography at her house. Between us, there were no quarrels over who would play what. I cast myself as the lover-boy and Priya as the lover who broke my heart. The slow dance embodied the push-pull of the song—coming together and pushing away from each other, the love and the hurt.

A few weeks later, we were performing in the gymnasium to a full room of joyous parents and kids, exuberantly cheering on each performance, whether it was their child or someone else's. Carrying a rose between my teeth, I whisked Priya around the stage, dramatically emphasizing the emotional agony with my facial expressions. The whirls and the dips punctuated by our proud glances at each other, hearing the crowd oohing and aahing over our moves. In the end, the performance was met with a crowd on their feet, clapping for us as we each took a bow. Mom, of course, waving at me and clapping the loudest in the back.

There were no questions or qualms about the two of us being girls, dancing together. Neither of us proclaiming, "I don't want to be the boy!" Or "I have to be the girl!" Nor were there students poking fun at us. There was only the joy and pleasure of dancing with Priya, and the satisfaction of our efforts being rewarded and acknowledged. Even afterwards, we were met with nothing but celebration. Parents and teachers commented on what a great show we'd put on. My mother gazing proudly at me as each shared some variation of "You should be so proud to have a daughter like this."

Over the coming months, the elation transmuted into disappointment when I learned we were moving north, to another suburb of Toronto—Richmond Hill. Yara had convinced our parents that it would be safer and cleaner there. In the last two years, our building's management had changed, and with that, significant issues arose—most notably, a rodent infestation that left us sleeping with one eye open.

I was disappointed at having to leave Scarborough behind, as well as beloved friends like Priya. Mom was disappointed, too. Both of us had grown to see it as home. After eleven years, it was the longest Mom had lived in one place, with the exception of her childhood home. And it was the only home I had memories in. When Yara wasn't around, I could overhear Mom venting to Khaleh Sima on the phone. She was convinced that it was more about how it looked for Yara to be living in Scarborough than it was about safety. Since being headhunted to work at a high-end boutique, Yara was noticeably different. She seemed more and more fixated on moving us out of Scarborough, as if our neighbourhood was no longer a respectable place to live.

Sometimes it felt like Yara held more power in our family than our own mother, especially now, as a twenty-one-year-old. She had an overwhelming amount of responsibility: financially contributing to the home, translating documents, filling out forms, helping me with my studies. And now, there was the added responsibility of helping my dad with his pipe dream of starting a transportation company. I got the sense that we *needed* Yara. Like my parents' acquiescence to her desires came less from agreement and more from knowing they couldn't financially float our life without her.

With all three of them working, we were still just barely able to afford a three-bedroom condo in Richmond Hill. It felt luxurious to have our own rooms, a gate out front where guests would check in, a pristine lobby and, my favourite, a hotel we shared amenities with. Staying away from the city centre or urban areas meant the mortgage was lower, especially given that there was very little around us by foot, aside from offices, an event space and a few restaurants.

That summer, with me newly isolated, Yara would take me in to work with her some days. She would set me up at the bakery across the way, where I'd quietly nibble on cheesecake and read books. During her breaks, she would walk over, making sure I had all the food and drinks I needed. With Yara's new job, I was noticing the emergence of a hyper-feminine aesthetic and high-fashion tastes. It was hard to imagine that my sister had ever played softball or floor hockey, or gone camping. Whereas before, jeans and a t-shirt would do, now it was leather jackets, body-hugging dresses and often heels. Sometimes, we would walk through the mall and I would notice how men would stare at her, their eyes tracing her face, quietly vying for her attention. It validated my own recognition of how beautiful my sister was. I wondered if she even realized how often it happened. If she did, she never once acknowledged it.

Sometimes, I would meander into the store, following Yara around as she taught me how to fold clothes the "right way"— something I would never learn to do—or read books on the comfy chairs when it was quiet. Men would take their time shopping with Yara, following her around the store as she picked out suit jackets and dress shirts. The way they looked at her, the emerging redness in their cheeks, telltale signs of their admiration.

The more time I spent with Yara, the more I longed to be like her. To walk through the world being so undeniably beautiful, so desirable and wanted that it excited others *just* to be around her. There was a quiet hope in me that with time, I would look like Yara. I had looked like a carbon copy of her in my early years, so it felt plausible.

With my father gone so often and Mom working more hours, Yara had become a second parent of sorts. On the first day of junior high school, she drove me there in her bright-red sedan—the windows down and the radio booming with pop music. My nerves grew as I walked towards the school, where kids clustered in tight groups and teachers, sectioned off by grades and with clipboards in hand, called out the names of their students. When none of the teachers called my name, it felt like the first sign that I didn't belong there. Yara marched over to a teacher and exchanged a few words, and within minutes, they pulled out a pen, wrote my name on the clipboard and welcomed me to their class.

The first day wasn't so bad after that. I mostly spent it on my own, observing the others reconnecting with friends after the summer break. On day two, I could hear the snickering behind me. The quiet whispers when I walked into rooms. Eventually, as the week went on, one of the Persian kids tapped me on my shoulder. Excited, I turned around, feeling finally noticed by someone.

"Hey, you know Amir?"

"Uhh . . . No."

"You sure you don't know Amir?"

"Yeah."

"Well, you look like Amir."

"Uh, okay."

I turned back around, deflated.

"She looks like a boy," I heard another whisper. People *were* noticing me, but only because I looked like a boy they knew. Sinking into my chair, I wished I was back in Scarborough, where I didn't stick out like a sore thumb. Or perhaps more aptly, an ugly one.

Things were different here. In Scarborough, we were all a bunch of kids of colour from low-income families. Here, while the crowd was mostly racialized—a mix of predominantly Persian, Chinese and white kids—it felt different. The popular girls all seemed to have straightened hair, thin bodies and cool clothes. Their faces, their legs, their arms—hairless like seals. I felt newly envious of the kids who wore Nike shoes, or Adidas tracksuits. I hadn't felt that envy in our old neighbourhood, where we shopped at all the same places in our local mall—Zellers for clothes, Payless for shoes. As the weeks continued, the differences between us amplified. Their homes—well, they were the houses we would pass on the way in, on the school bus. Walking distance from the school, multi-floored and with driveways that could fit basketball hoops or hockey nets. Some of the kids were dropped off in luxury cars, like Mercedes or BMWs. While we had moved up in socio-economic class, the gap between me and the other kids was obvious to me.

In class, the whispers continued as the popular kids snickered and made comments under their breath about my sideburn hairs, which ran down my neck, or the thick hair on my arms, or my bushy eyebrows. It was often quiet, but relentless. I would retreat within myself until recess, when I could run to a bathroom stall and cry alone. The history teacher eventually noticed me retreating, and asked me to stay behind after class. When she asked me what was wrong, I felt an inkling of hope, like finally someone could help me.

"What's wrong, Roza?" she asked, with genuine concern in her face.

"The other kids make fun of me. They think I look like a boy."

"You know, sometimes boys are mean to girls, but it's because they like them. Have you ever heard of that?"

If there was any hope in me before, it felt zapped from my body. I was too old to believe that lie. I knew the difference between what I was going through and boys joking with the popular girls they found desirable. There, they would poke fun as a way to spark more conversation. Sometimes I would hear a rude joke, followed by a noncommittal compliment. Or a playful shove.

Their unkindness was not a sign of affection; it was a painful reminder that I was different. That I straddled the line between masculinity and femininity in a way that rendered me, at best, uncomfortably hyper-visible, and at worst, ugly and undesirable.

As my twelfth birthday approached, there was an ever-growing stack of presents by the window from my family. The first was a bright-blue popcorn shirt with flowers on it that I'd loved since seeing it at Walmart—my mom's doing, to remember such a thing. I immediately went to my room and put it on. Tummy exposed, a tight fabric that hugged my body. My fantasy about wearing it at school was quickly interrupted by Mom, who said I could only wear it around the house. "Too sexy," she said in English as she pulled the bottom down.

The other gifts were very obviously from my sister, who valued brand names and popular fashion. Yara had always shown care through gift-giving, but this year felt extravagant. Perhaps because of the bullying at school, there was extra motivation to deck me out in the most popular gear. One of the boxes was a pair of Nike high-tops, white and bright pink. There were white skates, too, and dresses, new shirts and jeans.

Yara wasn't one to talk about feelings. I sensed this was her way of helping, instead of talking about the bullying. Her idea being that if I could look better, the other kids would accept me, and that acceptance would ease their unkindness towards me. The logic made sense to me, given that this was her own story. Having been called a "boy" and bullied for her accent, her hair, her clothes, what ultimately gave her protection was changing herself, aesthetically, to align with what was popular. It was a belief that I was starting to internalize, willing to get behind anything that granted me relief from the barrage of disparaging comments whispered around me.

It felt like the worst thing someone could call me was a boy. The more they did, the more urgency I felt to prove my girlhood. I daydreamed all weekend about reintroducing myself as feminine. I strutted the pink Nikes in front of the long mirror in our living room, admiring how the glossy pink accents looked against my brown skin. I looked at my body in the tight blue shirt—how it showed off my newly emerging curves. There was a distinct feeling of pleasure in seeing myself as pretty. My cheeks radiant and my eyes beaming with the anticipation of others seeing me just as I was seeing myself.

On Monday, I buzzed with excitement as I boarded the bus, feeling like a different person. I spent the day hyper-fixated on the faces of others, trying to see if anyone would notice me. As the day progressed, I felt more and more deflated, realizing that no one looked at me any differently.

That nothing had changed fuelled my sense of desperation as I continued on the path, turning to Yara as a perfect case study. Even my family doctor had encouraged me to be more like my sister when I stepped on a scale, reminding me that her body was the "right" body, and mine was a work-in-progress. I learned from her as she prepared for work. Her hair blow-dried and straightened, with a gloss and shine that I envied. Her clothes form-fitting and feminine, often paired with heels.

I started straightening my hair, too. Yara reassured me that the gap between my teeth was something that could be fixed with braces. Something that I hadn't even considered as a problem. Most problems had easy fixes, especially under the guidance of Yara.

As time went on, there *were* things that changed. I made friends with a crew of kids that reminded me of my Scarborough friends, but even then, the bullying continued. That year, I begged Mom to let me come to a *sofreh* with her, and she agreed, letting me skip school for it. So little had changed when it came to boys and their whispering judgments about me. Having seen my mother turn to Muslim practices in her own hard times,

I did the same, hoping it would grant me some ease—and by "grant me ease," I meant make me pretty.

When I was growing up, Mom rarely prayed, and if she did, it was during times of great hardship, like when someone was sick or struggling back home. The one Muslim practice we consistently attended was a *sofreh-e nazri*. Called a sofreh for short, it was a gathering of women centred around food and prayer. Food was a ceremonial offering to spirits and Shia saints. Those hosting and attending would often arrive with a request already in their heart, hoping the spirits or saints would carry it to Allah for an answer.

At the door, we took our shoes off and were greeted by a group of aunties, some strangers, some family. We greeted each of them in the room, bowing our heads as a sign of respect and acknowledgement. To those we knew more dearly, two kisses on the cheek or, depending on where they were from in Iran, sometimes three. There were varying degrees of religiosity in the room. Some women prayed five times a day, from dawn to dusk. Some rarely prayed. Some wore hijabs and beautiful tunics, inside and outside the home. Some, like my mom, were dressed casually in jeans and a long-sleeved shirt, along with a hijab in hand for prayer.

In the kitchen, another set of aunties were lined up, waiting to stir something simmering in a large silver pot on the stove. I waited with Mom in line as she greeted others. When it was her turn, she handed me the wooden spoon and said, "Think of what you want, and stir." *I want the boys to be nice to me*, I thought. I worried that wasn't clear enough for God and started to list their names: *Ehsan, Farhad, Pouya*. I then worried that could be *any* Ehsan, Farhad and Pouya, so I started to visualize them as I stirred, wishing for them to find me pretty.

My mother waited quietly until I was done, unbothered by how long it took me. We crammed into the living room of thirty or so women sitting on chairs and around the sofreh. I took longer than usual to choose my spot, wanting to find the perfect *kachi* to sit near. A kachi was a sweet dish with a thick, pudding-type consistency. They were laid around the sofreh in Styrofoam bowls with a plate covering each one. When you opened the lid, it presented you with a visual that some, with special teachings, were able to read. Similar to reading the bottom of a Turkish coffee, or getting a Tarot reading. On the sofreh was also feta, bread, parsley and turnips. Mom and I put our hijabs on and waited.

When we were all seated, one woman began reading the suras in the Quran. The rhythmic nature of how it was read reminded me of a sad melody. I followed the other women, never knowing what to do at a sofreh. When some opened their palms on their thighs, mine opened. When they lifted their palms to the sky, I did the same. When some rocked, I rocked. Eventually, the women began crying. Not just any crying, but something deep, guttural. My mom, too. Tears streamed down her face. Napkins passed from one side of the sofreh to another. And I cried, too. If there was anywhere to cry, it was here. It was here that you could unburden yourself of the pain of living. It was here that others would rock with you, would cry with you, would fall apart. There was no shame here—only radical honesty. Soon, the whole room hummed with a symphony of sadness—crumpled tissues, the shaking in the chest as tears streamed uncontrollably, that hiccupping gasp when the snot started coming.

When the prayer was done, the requests for *salavat* (prayers/blessings) rolled in.

A prayer for the children living in poverty.
A prayer for my brother, who is sick at home, awaiting treatment.
A prayer for my child.
A prayer for my neighbour.

When the prayers and storytelling were over, women quickly took their kachi over to a particular auntie, one who often attended the sofreh. She was one of the few people who could read a kachi. First, she opened up the kachi and gazed at it as if piecing together what it was revealing to her. Then she would explain what she saw and what the person needed to do, if anything, to arrive into their hopes. For some, it was to host their own sofreh, while for others, it was to light a certain number of candles with heart-focus and intentionality.

When the auntie opened my kachi, her eyes widened. "Look how beautiful!" she exclaimed. "*Allah* is written on your kachi." She showed it to me, spelling out the letters and pointing to each one. Then she showed it to my mother, and soon, other women were gazing raptly at it, too. It felt like the confirmation I needed: that Allah was still there, protecting me. "There is nothing to be done here," she explained. "God is with you."

Getting invited to a birthday felt like a sign that God was, in fact, with me. The invite came from Shireen, who I'd met on my bus to school. We knew each other by circumstance. She lived in the condo building across from us and waited with me at the bus stop, along with her younger brother, in the mornings. Though Shireen was only one year older, she seemed like a teenager to me. Each of her eyebrows a thin, arched line that she maintained regularly. Her skin bronzed with makeup and blush. I would listen intently to her stories about her secret boyfriend—stories consisting, for the most part, of reviews of everyday conversations they'd had over MSN Messenger, a popular messaging app. Even so, it was titillating to listen to, making me feel like I was one step closer to the experience.

I spent the morning of her birthday picking out my best clothes and deciding whether my hair was best tucked behind my ears or left to frame my face. Arriving at the event room, I quickly took note of her brother, who was a spikier person, often poking fun at others. As the evening went on, he found his opportunity to poke fun at me, too, reminding me that I looked like a boy. Though it was a tired insult, my eyes still welled up each time it was uttered. Without thinking, I grabbed his shoulders and kneed him in the penis. He shrieked immediately, cupping his penis in his hands and yelling to his mother in a high-pitched, whiny voice, "She kicked me in the penis!" I denied the whole thing outright. His mother crouched down to him, holding his shoulders and explaining, "You know, she probably didn't mean to do it." Her eyes trying to meet mine. I quickly looked away. She knew, and I knew that she knew.

I had no guilt or shame about kneeing him in the penis. I felt he deserved it, as did all the other boys who were making fun of me. This was a different me, given that I had always clung to niceness, choosing to walk away and cry in private. Fighting back instead of shutting down and disappearing. I left the party after the debacle, wanting to avoid any retaliation.

In the days that followed the party, I uttered a lie that quickly snowballed into another lie, a sinking into this new version of myself. It started when, one morning, Shireen arrived at the bus stop distraught over the end of her relationship. I felt empathy for her—she was clearly struggling with the heartache of it all, but I was also curious about the experience. Boys and girls had begun openly pairing up in my class, and it felt like I was on the outside, watching everyone have these dreamy experiences that were utterly inaccessible to anyone who looked like me. No matter how hard I tried, I was no closer to any of it.

On the way home that day, sitting next to Shireen again, I blurted out, "I have a cousin who likes you." I didn't. "You do?" she responded, her face perking up with excitement. "What's his name?" she asked, leaning in closer. "Arman," I lied. "You should add him . . . No, he'll add you. I'll talk to him," I reassured her. Instead of backtracking, I dug myself deeper into the hole. I went home and created an MSN Messenger account for "Arman." Pulled an image from Google of someone who could pass as my cousin and added Shireen, who immediately started chatting with me.

This went on for a couple weeks. I would sign on as Arman and flirt with Shireen about how pretty I found her, and how I missed her during the days when we couldn't talk. Seeing her name pop up on my screen would exhilarate me. Passing questions back and forth, I finally felt like the others. We would talk about simple things, like how our days had gone, or what songs we were listening to. The next day, Shireen would tell me about her affection for Arman, and I would beam, knowing we were one and the same.

Amidst it all, I forgot that I was doing anything wrong. The line between reality and fantasy was thinning. Ironically, it felt easier to be Arman than myself. Being a girl had felt exhausting. To me, girlhood was no more than a constant fixation with changing oneself to appear more feminine and less masculine. Being Arman was just being me. The only differences between us were the name, the fake picture and his love of soccer, an added detail that felt important at the time, to distinguish myself as a boy.

Briefly, I got to be myself. Well, sort of. However selfish it was, I got to play in the garden, like everyone else my age. I got to lust for someone who lusted for me. I got to feel the excitement of seeing her name pop up on my screen, and experience the genuine curiosity as we asked each other questions back and forth. I got to feel the joy of wanting and being wanted, to bask in the sweetness of our compliments. Briefly, I belonged to someone. I had created a world where all the experiences that were inaccessible to me in the real world were suddenly available to me. A world where I was accepted, safe and even desired.

As things became more serious, the pressure to meet Shireen

in person loomed heavily. Eventually, I told her that Arman had moved away and could no longer talk to her. When she pressed me for more information, obviously upset about it ending so abruptly, the truth came out—that it was me, the whole time, catfishing her. Instead of being angry with me, she was deeply embarrassed and ashamed to have fallen for my ruse, which felt much worse. I had hurt someone who had done nothing to deserve it. In fact, I liked Shireen. She was one of the first and few people who had been kind to me at the new school.

My overwhelming instinct was to move on, as quickly as I could, with no reminders of what had transpired between us. I wanted to pretend it hadn't happened at all. In the days that followed, Shireen didn't look at me anymore, and I didn't look at her, either. Neither of us said hello in the mornings, our eyes glued to the concrete instead as we waited for the bus. I longed for the summer, when she would graduate and move on to high school. I wanted desperately for her to disappear. To rid myself of the memory of her entirely. A memory that made me so uncomfortable, I wanted to peel myself from my own skin.

The catfish fiasco solidified my belief that I was just too ugly. This time, the ugliness had spread to my spirit, too. I felt certain that if God had been with me before, God wasn't with me now—loathing me as much as I loathed myself. Standing in front of the mirror, I saw a monstrous reflection looking back at me—hairy-bodied, belly hanging over my jeans, a beak-like nose. *Maybe you* are *a boy*, I told myself in a taunting voice, wincing as I remembered what had happened with Shireen.

I declared myself ugly again and again, my whip-like tongue engraving it in my skin. It was easier to feel the shame of my body—to taunt myself for all the ways I failed to be a girl—than to reckon with the pain of rejection and un-belonging.

7

HAM-DARD

I was fourteen years old when my aversion towards my father deepened. It wasn't that his behaviour towards me changed, but rather, that I had become more conscious of his hurtful behaviour towards my mother. He'd begun to remind me of the absurdly inept husbands in sitcoms like *Everybody Loves Raymond* and *The King of Queens* that my mother and I watched night after night. We'd laugh until our eyes watered and we were bent over, holding our bellies in pain. By 10 p.m., Mom would be asleep, waking only from the sound of me getting up for bed.

While there were parallels to these characters, Dad's attitude had stopped being comical to me. The chauvinistic man blubbering about, making mistake after mistake and laughing it off. Unable to do anything without his wife, either, all the while diminishing her with his sexist commentary.

At family gatherings, I braced myself for the humiliation ritual that was sure to ensue, knowing something terrible would inevitably roll off Dad's tongue. It began with minor slights about my mother before he would inevitably say, "One day, I'm going to find myself an Afghan wife." The men gathered around him would then turn to my mother, their deep belly laugher ricocheting off the walls. I rolled my eyes at him and turned to my mom, who I felt increasingly protective of. I could see her pretending not to hear it. The men, not taking the hint, would start yelling "Mina Khanoom, did you hear that?" Eventually, she would throw her hands up with a grin, chuckle and refocus on her own conversations with the women there. It was a brilliant performance. Her discomfort temporarily concealed. But I could see through it, feeling sadness for my mother, who smiled through it all, trying to preserve her dignity.

On some days, he would replace "Afghan wife" with "Filipina wife," but the sentiment remained the same. My whole body shuddered and recoiled in response to his tired jokes, embarrassed that *that* was my father. I wasn't too young to know there was something jarring and gross about it all. I later found language for it, realizing the racism and misogyny of perceiving Afghan and Filipino women as the embodiment of duty. This is what all the slights and jokes boiled down to: my mother not being dutiful *enough*. My mother, who gave every ounce of herself to running our household smoothly while my father was away, all the while working a full-time job. There was nothing more enraging than watching my mother torn down in public; to me, she was the epitome of *good*. I now understood, more than before, why my sisters so often scoffed and eye-rolled at my father.

That year, I briefly thought the tides were changing with my father when he finally gave my mother what she always wanted: a house. It was the grand romantic gesture none of us were expecting, given how little intimacy existed between them. None of us could make sense of how he could afford to buy a house, either, but it didn't matter then. Instead of questioning it all, Mom and I pored over pictures of the new development, excited by the prospect of a backyard with a garden. I was mostly excited for my mom, who stared in awe at the large, white-framed windows and the peach hue of the brick exteriors. To her, a house was a symbol of success that all her immigrant peers had already acquired. And now, after years of hard work in a garment factory, it was her turn, too.

I thought it was a good omen when the move brought the whole family back together again. Yasaman was still with her boyfriend, and after just having had a baby, asked if they could move in temporarily until they had enough money saved up. Yara took the room next to Yasaman's, continuing to live with us and help support the mortgage. And I moved into the smallest room, with just enough space for a bed and desk.

Our first summer in the home, Mom started planting her garden. There wasn't much to the backyard, but having one at all reignited her joy. She planted herbs for the first time: mint, dill, parsley and cilantro. Some weekends, she would stand in the kitchen, looking meditative as she cleaned her herbs. First, setting them in a bowl of water, draining it and doing it again, until the water was clean enough. Second, picking off the leaves from the stems, delicately, one by one. With the sun glistening on her face, I was reminded of her and Baba Ali sitting quietly in the courtyard, cleaning their herbs. I wondered if that was where she went, too.

Yara now worked as an office receptionist and was continuing a sociology degree at the university, taking a few courses at a time. Her favourite class had become one focused on Indigenous communities. She would passionately describe colonialism and its impacts on Indigenous people, who, she reminded me, were still living on this land. I listened quietly, absorbing her passion as much as her knowledge about Indigenous sovereignty and treaty rights.

It was exciting to see a different Yara emerging through all her learning—a politicized side to her slowly growing. The more Yara read, the more her protective spirit started to change shape—embracing not just us, the family, but other communities, too. More and more, she took an interest in supporting Indigenous rights and resistance. I liked this version of her better than the Yara of my preteens, whose conversations had felt limited to how I looked and how I dressed. Though remnants of that still popped up, like comments about my jiggly belly or growing moustache.

While I was in hopeful spirits, Yasaman had become convinced the home was haunted. She was always sensing ghosts and spirits. Frozen in fear, she would see a bloodied little girl sitting at the end of her bed. Or the shadow of an older woman standing at the door. In this house, it was a man standing by the window, but it was too dark to make out his face. She invited over her boyfriend's mom, a God-fearing Christian woman, to "cleanse" the space. Apparently, after that, he was gone. Truth be told, I'm not convinced it was her boyfriend's mom that did it. I think even the ghost could see a storm coming in that house.

No one—with the exception of the ghost—could've known that a year and a half later, it would feel like a vacuum sealer had sucked the joy out of our home. It wouldn't be hyperbolic to say that everyone was changed by it, as were our relationships. It started with my mother finding a condom in my father's wallet. She had gotten her tubes tied years before, and to her, there was only one reason her fifty-five-year-old husband would carry a condom around in his wallet. Though he denied it all, whatever bond had been left between them quickly died.

Dad started sleeping on the couch every time he returned from his trips, until eventually, he stopped coming home. I never asked where he went, because I didn't want to know. It already felt like I knew too much. When he was gone, Mom would sob. Most of the time, I said the only thing it felt right to say: "You should leave, Mom. You deserve better."

I avoided thinking about my father altogether. The idea of him being sexually intimate with another person felt overwhelmingly disgusting. Even his voice started to repulse me, so I avoided the phone when his name flashed across it. Instead of feeling grief, I felt nothing. I continued going to school, except now, I could barely remember anything from my classes. For long stretches of time, I disappeared into a twilight zone of nothingness—a fuzziness that I would float towards and suddenly be zapped out of by the sound of the bell. An old teacher of mine stopped me in the hallway one day, looked deeply into my eyes and said, "You used to be so happy—always a big smile on your face." Maybe the joy had been sucked out of our home *and* me.

When I thought things couldn't get worse, they did. Yara had to file for bankruptcy. Dad had blown through her credit cards for his aspirational transportation business, which had ultimately failed. He was so behind on his monthly payments that we had regular visits from people demanding their money at our door. Eventually, Yara made a conclusive decision: we were moving out. Yasaman and her family moved out, too, finding a place further north of us, an hour away. We'd rarely see her anymore.

Since Mom couldn't afford a place on her own, Yara continued living with us, the three of us cramped into a two-bedroom basement unit. Yara and I in one bedroom, like our Scarborough years, Mom in the other. The place reminded me of a hospital, white-walled with cold fluorescent lighting. Three tiny windows—a few inches to remind you that the outside world existed. With the landlord controlling the heat, we bundled up and lived under blankets to stay warm.

A couple weeks after the move, Mom and I returned to the old house to pick up some boxes in the garage. Seeing that the lights were on in the living room, we walked curiously up the steps and pressed our faces against the front door window, hands cupped around our eyes and our mouths steaming up the glass. Where there were once couches and a coffee table were now two mattresses with two women we'd never seen before sitting atop of them. We were both thinking it—one of these women was *the* woman. The one my father had cheated on my mother with, and clearly moved on with.

My mother stayed magnetically pressed against the window in the door, frozen. Wanting to shield her, I grabbed at her hands and tried to pull her away. "Mom, let's go," I pleaded with her repeatedly. Instead, her fingers gripped at the door more tightly, her eyebrows furrowed. "That was my living room," she mumbled, with tears filling her eyes. "It was mine." The last time I remembered hearing those words was in Iran, after leaving my uncle's home. The memory of my grandmother and aunt holding her flashed before me. I tried to suck back the hot tears streaming from my eyes as I grabbed her hands, trying desperately to pull her away. All the sadness I hadn't allowed myself to feel poured out. I was feeling the grief it all: of losing my home, of watching the family fall apart, of my father abandoning us. Eventually, Mom lowered her hands, got into the car and drove us away for the last time.

When the winter came, both my mother and Yara went into hibernation. Yara, who had just started to be so passionate about her studies and to share them with me, disappeared. She left school and started working longer hours. When she was home, she was ghostly—sleeping, or watching television while gazing into the distance, somewhere else entirely. Mom, who was once joyful and warm and kind, disappeared, too. Crawled into a den of her own making, the leaves and the snow obscuring her body.

Mom had become emotionally volatile, leaving me unsure of who I would get each day. The day she was granted full custody of me was the day I started to notice we were no longer quite the same. Mom's lawyer had prepared the documents, and when the question of child support came up, my father laughed and responded with "What money?" "This was the only day in our entire lives that your father showed up early, pen in hand: the day he had to sign you away," Mom said to me, casually, with a laugh. As painful as it was to hear how easily my father could leave me behind, it was just as painful to hear the cold words roll off her tongue.

"God, I can't even look at you. You look like your dad," she would say on other days, her nose scrunched up as if physically ill at the sight of my face. My face was no longer neutral in the way it had been, or endearing, as it once was when I was a child. Unable to see her olive skin and round face in me, instead, all Mom could see in my face was my dad's thinly stretched-out almond eyes. This was new to me—feeling rejected by her, abandoned by her. The separation had been like two countries brutally dividing. That I had fallen within her borders had felt right. Yet I felt unclaimed by her. In the unbearable, growing distance between us, I wanted to wake her, to shake her body and remind her that it was *me*, her daughter. To remind of her of who we used to be. Her, a perched hawk. Me, the one she had always protected so fiercely.

On other days, Mom was a fragile being who fell apart in ways that tugged at my whole heart. One day, she was getting ready to drive me to school at 7:30 a.m. First, in the kitchen, packing my lunch into two containers—one with a sandwich, one with fruit. Then in my room, hurrying me to get my things together and leave. It had been snowing heavily the night before, so we were rushing to leave early enough.

She turned on the car, blasted the heat and had me sit in the warmth as she cleaned off the snow with her brush. The streets were empty, with a few cars sliding around on the main street, trying to make it through the slush. Mom went to the front of the car and tried to put the windshield wipers back down. Then I heard a snap, and a second snap. I looked up and saw my mom with a windshield wiper in each hand, tears streaming down her face. I watched as her whole body collapsed onto the front hood. I stayed inside the car—crying with her. Wanting to ease her pain, but not knowing how.

Khaleh Sima was waiting for us at a nearby Tim Hortons, halfway between her house and ours. Where we'd once gathered in homes and parks or around a sofreh, now we hung around a table at a chain coffee shop. In the past, I'd thought it was sad to hang around coffee shops at night, where it was mostly seniors and solo middle-aged people. That teenage judgment dissipated when it became our weekly refuge, too. At seven o'clock in the evening, we drove over to the parking lot with Persian music blaring in the car. Both of us immediately felt more life in our bodies, excited to see Khaleh Sima, who would inevitably make us laugh amidst our despair.

Khaleh Sima was the only friend my mother still held on to and the only one she could be her full, unfiltered self with. She was what Persians would call *ham-dard*, meaning one's companion in pain. Mom's other friends had slowly disappeared. At first, there was empathy. A couple even shared that they knew of my father's infidelities from spotting him with other women, or thinking they had. Or that they'd heard he had been calling other women in our circle. But the phone calls from these friends stopped, and I wasn't sure if it was her distancing or theirs.

Outside the Tim Hortons, teenage lovers leaned against car doors, canoodling, and I just hoped no one from my school would spot me. Though no one would have said much about it anyway, given that I was rarely, if ever, invited to parties. Groups of twenty-somethings waited by their cars for their box of pizza. And solo middle-aged men would be sitting in their cars, waiting, too. For what? I never quite knew.

By the cash register, Mom and Khaleh Sima argued over who would pay this time. Each of them pulling out their debit cards like swords and jousting with their hands. The two went back and forth, swearing they wouldn't let the other person pay or promising that they'd never go out with them again, until one eventually gave up and let the other pay. It was a form of tarof, a practice of politeness, to battle over payment. I found it both endearing and comedic, as did the coffee shop staff, who waited and smiled as if they knew the dance well.

As soon as we sat down, the two of them started venting about their lives, taking breaks only to sip their tea. My ears perked up as Mom vented about Dad, cursing his lineage for his very existence; Khaleh Sima, mirroring Mom's rage, cursed his existence, too. I sat there silently eating my Boston cream donut, fascinated by the creativity of the Persian language. It wasn't just what was said, but how it was said. Mom would repeat the words once spoken by Dad and curse at him as if he was in the room with us. "*Khak to saret*," she would say, meaning "Dirt on your head." Or "*Zahre mar*," meaning "Eat snake poison." Or my personal favourite, "*Shashidam tu ruhet*," meaning "I pissed in your soul." That one, Mom would apologize for after saying it, as if it crossed the line of "too inappropriate."

There were so many ways to curse someone, all of which felt more cutting than the words we had in English. And sometimes more hilarious, especially when I translated them into English for myself. As the two moved through rage, they made it to another side—one with more levity and humour. By the end, Khaleh Sima was sharing stories from her week, mostly about ridiculous encounters she'd had with others. Sometimes she would directly translate Farsi words into English at random, and we would be nearly rolling on the floor laughing. "I said . . . why are you looking at me left-left," she once said—a very literal translation from the Persian phrase "*chap chap*," referencing when someone is glaring or scowling at you. Both Mom and I would be in tears laughing, and Mom would beg her to stop, waving her hands and cry-yelling, "I'm going to pee."

There was a growing desire in me to get accepted to a university in another town and move away. I wanted to free Mom and Yara from the responsibility of caring for me, of putting a roof over my head and food on my plate. Surprisingly, both my sister and my mother were in immediate agreement. When my sisters were younger, my mother had refused to let them leave town for university or college, fearing that their independence would lead to trouble with men. They were too young, she felt. This time around, without hesitation, she said, "I don't want you to end up like Yara, tied up with us." Her eyes pleading with me to leave, as if at some point it would be too late. A cage door would suddenly close and I would be trapped with them. Now I think we all wanted the same thing for each other: to be free.

Over time, I had become Mom's confidante again—her *ham-dard*. Validating her feelings, echoing her anger, confirming her story again and again. The story being, mostly, that Dad was the root of all evil. "Yes, Dad is the devil," I echoed her. Instinctually, I knew what to say. The words oozed out of me like honey. It was how I could cocoon her, protecting her as she healed from the heaviness of her heartache. To create a soft landing for all her hard feelings, by being in her pain *with* her. Night after night, I held her rage and let it disintegrate into grief—and sometimes, even, a glimmer of acceptance.

There was a delicate balance to the relationship we had just re-established. She had begun warming up to me again, but any mention of my own sadness seemed to trigger the sudden emergence of the colder part of her. Her favourite phrase: "Why sad? Don't be." When I had a quiet yearning for my father, it only felt right to crush it. An inner voice would remind me that there was no room for me to miss him. Missing him was a betrayal of my mother. She was, after all, the one who actually wanted me, and how dare I miss the man who hurt her.

Instead, I sought a soft landing elsewhere, knowing my mother just couldn't be *that* mother for me right now. That year, I signed up for a writing course in which Mr. Surrey, the teacher, introduced us to Ani DiFranco's music. Mr. Surrey was the quintessential image of the English teacher: a thirty-something white dude with shoulder-cut wavy hair, oversized glasses and Birkenstocks. Girls at the school swooned over his dramatic poetry readings, his baritone voice, his love of marginalia. During lunchtimes, he sat solo in his car, smoking and listening to Dave Matthews Band.

In class, we took a magnifying glass to Ani DiFranco's lyrics and delicately picked apart her genius. There was something delicious about her rage. How her sharp tongue would gut Western imperialism like a fish. She talked about people and places others were afraid to talk about with any empathy—Afghanistan, Iraq, Palestine. Then there was Sylvia Plath. A month into our introduction, I had memorized the words of her poem "Daddy," where she wrote ragefully about patriarchy and her own relationship with her father. Every recitation felt like the purging of something too painful to name out loud as my own.

Over time, performing someone else's rage made room for my own unspoken anger. I bought a beautiful notebook with an ornate cover from the local bookstore—brown with a gold design and a clasp to close it. I came to women writers wanting to learn to write, but perhaps I was trying to find a place for all the feelings I kept bottling up inside. At night, I climbed onto my bed and bled rage all over its pages. The notebook became my *ham-dard*, my soft landing. The pages inviting me to feel *all* my feelings, promising to have patience, compassion and space for me. And so I just kept returning to my notebook, putting my feelings down and watching them shift from rage to grief to acceptance and back to rage again. Each time walking away a little bit lighter.

On Friday nights, we would drive over to our local video store, Blockbuster, to pick up a few movies. The parking lot of the plaza packed with families, and dates, and singles also headed the same way. It was *the* place to be, and there was no shame for me in being there with Mom. In fact, I looked forward to our Friday nights. Mom and I beelined to the romantic comedies, picking up two or three for the weekend—like *How to Lose a Guy in 10 Days* or *Sleepless in Seattle*. On occasion, Yara wanted in on movie night, too. Usually that meant an action movie or a thriller was sure to make the list, something with Jason Statham or Paul Walker. We walked down the aisle of sugary and salty treats, loading up on chocolate and chips. My go-to the chocolate-covered raisins that made me feel like we were going to the theatre.

At home, I popped in the movie for the night, *Just Friends*, and pressed pause. Yara gathered blankets for the inevitable moment we would all start shivering and Mom would curse our landlord, who kept the heat to a frigid minimum. I could hear Mom from the living room, frying up some spinach for Yara's favourite—*mast-e esfenaj*, meaning "yogurt and spinach": a simple combination of cooked spinach folded into yogurt with some salt and pepper. Coming into the living room, she squeezed herself onto the couch with the giant bowl of *mast-e esfenaj*. We turned off the lights and the three of us crowded under the pile of blankets. Passed the bag of chips back and forth, dipping them into the bowl and savouring the salty flavour.

"You crunch so loud," Yara whispered at me, as she used to, her eyes looking annoyed. There was strange comfort in the familiarity of her being annoyed with me. A familiarity that had disappeared for a while, after our move into the basement. Most of the week, Mom looked tired, dragging herself to her minimum-wage factory job for nine hours a day and then coming home to prepare dinner. But on movie night, there was a lightness about her that told me she was coming out of hibernation, back to her regular *Mom* self. By the end of the movie, Mom was sleeping on the couch, only woken by the sound of me singing Boyz II Men's "I Swear" from the movie. Yara laughing at my face as I dramatically and expressively opened and closed my eyes, stretching my mouth to exaggerate each word. The fact that we could still laugh reminded me that there was more than pain and heartache in this home; there was still love.

8

UGLY

I was seventeen when I left home for university. A few hundred dollars in my pocket, and a lot of hope that this would be the year everything would change for me. That suddenly boys would look at me and think, *My god she's beautiful*, and we'd fall in love, then be pulled apart by circumstances beyond our control, only to find each other again and marry in our late twenties. In ways, it was similar to the fantasy I'd tried to play out in middle school with Shireen, except this time, I would be myself and it would be real.

Mom had enthusiastically volunteered to drive me to Wilfrid Laurier University, which was in Waterloo. The decision to attend Laurier was an easy one: It was the only school with a Communications program that was within a couple of hours drive from Toronto. At the time I was convinced I would be the next Samantha Jones from *Sex and the City*. For weeks prior, in every phone call to family in Iran, she'd found ways to weave in the fact that I was off to university. Her voice projected loudly into the phone, as if alerting our entire neighbourhood. She relished seeing me pursue higher education. "It's all I ever wanted," she would tell me. And I relished her joy. To her, it didn't matter what I was studying or where I was going. All that mattered was that I was attending university—something neither my mom nor her sisters had the opportunity to do.

Driving through Waterloo, I felt the urge to cover Mom's eyes. White boys with beer cans in hand, mismatched lawn chairs out, poster boards with messily handwritten "HONK IF YOU HAVE DAUGHTERS!" I was lucky that my immigrant mother was driving and couldn't read fast enough in English to catch their drift. Like Christmas-season nativity scenes, iterations of the same spectacle appeared across multiple streets until we arrived at my dorm.

Though my mother witnessed the spectacle, she never once asked questions or seemed concerned about me. She held firmly and unflinchingly to the belief that her daughter was above it all. A good Muslim girl who would never, ever dare drink alcohol, kiss a boy or stay up late. This good-girl image was so ingrained that no one in my family had thought to give me "the talk." Mom never spoke of sex—for fear, I imagine, that speaking about it would unwittingly encourage it. My father and Yasaman had mostly disappeared in the last couple of years. And Yara still saw me as her near-invisible, chubby, bush-faced younger sister.

When I arrived at the residence apartment, Jennifer peered out of the kitchen with a bright, beaming smile. Jennifer was my roommate—a tall, thin-bodied woman with freckled white skin, long ginger hair and deep-green eyes. "We don't have anything for coffee, but my mom can get us a coffee machine. Company benefits," she explained. "Is it cool if we have a party tonight?" she asked, barely waiting for a response. I wasn't about to say no. I was *dying* for my first "college party" experience.

By sundown, groups of white men were pouring into our apartment, each with a bottle of liquor in hand. Some tall and chiselled—probably athletes, I thought. Some resembling characters out of the TV show *The O.C.*—bad-boy chic, like Ryan, or cute and nerdy like beloved Seth. Most wore some version of blue jeans and a white t-shirt or a band t-shirt.

Immediately, they set up beer pong at our kitchen table and started pulling out red cups.

Jennifer's friends all resembled each other in some way. Thin-bodied white girls in jean shorts and tank tops, with variations only in their colouring—bleach-blondes, or natural redheads, or dark-haired with piercing blue eyes. Some gathered in the kitchen and downed shots of vodka. Some joined the boys in playing beer pong.

There were three or four of us folks of colour—all sticking out like misplaced puzzle pieces. Looking around, I felt a steep sense of unbelonging and a thumping desire to make them like me. When some of Jennifer's friends realized I had no drink, they asked if I wanted something from their bottles. When I told them I'd never drunk alcohol or smoked and wouldn't be nineteen until next year, they all found it rather endearing. "Oh, you're a straight-edge," one of them said to me. "A straight-edge?" I asked. "Yeah, you know, goody-goody, you don't drink, you don't smoke, shit like that." And though it was true, I couldn't help but want to shake that title as fast as I could. I didn't want to be a straight-edge; I wanted to be sexy, and desired, and fun. I wanted to be one of them.

As I watched boys invite them to play beer pong, or flirt with them over their smooth ability to take shots in one go, or tug at their waists, envy brewed inside of me.

Campus was the first time I'd found myself in a predominantly white place. Sometimes, I was one of two brown people in a class. I realized quickly that there were a hundred kinds of white woman you could be. The Ugg-boots-and-jean-skirts type. The ones with floral dresses from small boutique stores, or big hipster glasses and side-parted pink hair, or university athletic gear with a ponytail. Maybe even the punk-band t-shirts and Doc Martens kind. It wasn't long before I realized that I, who'd dreamed of this kind of freedom last year, was mostly invisible to this small-town, country-listening crowd. That as it turned out, being a *dokhtar Irooni* (Iranian girl)—a brown-skinned, hairy-armed, chubby Iranian girl—didn't do it for the suburban boys back home or the small-town boys here.

When I asked my mother what she'd dreamed of at seventeen, she responded: "I was ugly. I didn't dream." Matter-of-fact, like saying the earth is round. Or perhaps more apt, the earth is flat.

She had absolved herself of the common dreams of girlhood, not daring to dream of romance, weddings, marriage; no, she relinquished it all early to dream a more suitable dream for unpretty girls like herself. She dreamed, instead, of education and religious duty. What she lacked in beauty, she would make up for in smarts and morals. She would be good at being good, she thought.

The list of what she didn't like about her face, her body, was ever-growing. Mom had small eyes, and vehemently hated how they made her look like a bird-eyed girl, two dots drawn onto a Jacobin cuckoo. She had a nose that dared bend and fold like the sand dunes of Dasht-e Kavir. A winding road of a nose that mapped generations of arch-nosed women and men. Her *sabze*—olive-toned—skin was amongst her greatest sources of shame, a darker shade of brown that only I had inherited. And a paper-thin body that she wished could fold itself into a teeny-tiny piece of origami and fly her far away.

When her aunties would visit her home, Mom and her siblings would rush to the front door, line up and greet them with kisses on both cheeks. One by one, the aunties would marvel at her sisters—their fair skin, wide eyes, plump bodies. When they came to her, they would say: "*Azizam*—dear one—your heart is so beautiful. Why couldn't your face be beautiful, too?" Mom would pause, swallowing the tears back into her body the way she always did, instinctually. Over time, she sought refuge in her room, away from the gaze of her aunties. "Better they not see me at all," she sighed.

She wasn't like the rest of her siblings. The others had bodies that were emblematic of the kind of possibility and promise beauty held for young women of their age. Mom and I weren't so different from one another. We both felt so profoundly unpretty that it became a debt we were always trying to balance. Always compensating for our aesthetic shortcomings by making ourselves small and agreeable.

"We would've been the pretty ones during the Qajar dynasty, you know?" I joked with Mom, both of us letting out a big chuckle before fading into quiet sorrow. Humour had become a way to ease the pain of our undesirability. But no matter how much we laughed, it never fully eclipsed the sadness.

For Iranians, the legacy of modernization, imperialism and colonialism—amongst other intersecting systems—had shifted our beauty standards to align with Europeans and whiteness during the 1900s. But before then, there was a radically different aesthetic. During the Qajar dynasty in the late 1800s, women with thick eyebrows and moustaches were deemed so beautiful that those with only faint moustaches would use mascara to paint darker wisps of hair above their lips. You could be gorgeously brown, and hairy, and fat. You could have hair that climbed your neck like lush ivy. Gloriously thick calves and ankles. A face so round it rivalled the sun. In other words, we would've been hot shit during the Qajar dynasty days.

But that wasn't her reality, and it sure wasn't mine. All those Fridays watching rom-coms with Mom had confirmed a few things. One, that neither of us was the standard of "pretty." We looked nothing like the main characters of the movies, with our tanned olive skin, our thin, almond-shaped eyes, our now round bodies. If we didn't go to the Persian salon every few weeks, my eyebrows would double in size and my moustache would grow out, as would the sideburn hairs that ran down my neck. My running self-deprecating joke was that though I had ample hair on my face and neck, somehow the hair on my head was thinning—barely a handful there for ponytails. Mom, on the other hand, had thick, dense curls that often blow-dried frizzy. No matter how hard we tried, we could never mirror the blowouts of the main characters, with their silky hair that swayed so effortlessly.

The rom-com industry had done exceptionally well in convincing girls and women like me that acquiring "pretty" status was not only doable, but a necessary step towards becoming a human worthy of love, belonging and dignity. This was the entire plot of *She's All That*, right? Freddie Prinze Jr. is dumped by his girlfriend in his senior year, and his friend, Paul Walker, bets that he can turn any girl into a prom queen (read: pretty and popular). He picks Rachael Leigh Cook, a near-invisible nerd. With the help of new hair, clothing and makeup, she transforms into a pretty, popular girl with a real chance at the crown.

Iterations of this plot exist across countless teen comedies, all with leading white women who in more ways than one already meet the standard of "pretty": white, thin, able-bodied, clear-skinned. Hilary Duff puts on a mask and a wedding dress in *A Cinderella Story* and is suddenly pretty and desirable to Chad Michael Murray. Anne Hathaway plucks her eyebrows and straightens her hair in *The Princess Diaries* to suddenly become royalty, worthy of reverence. This was the same plot Yara had tried to sell me in my preteens, having lived it in some form during her own youth.

The promise of love and acceptance obscured the fact that this fantasy was bullshit, especially to many women and girls of colour. As hard as I tried to assimilate into white girlhood, I would always be merely a mimic—a brown girl cosplaying whiteness. The promise was just that for brown girls like me—a perpetual promise that kept us vying. Though some part of me knew this, I still tried, and each time I failed, I blamed myself for not having tried hard enough. The shame and self-loathing of my twelve-year-old self, still alive in me.

Whiteness became a performance I studied with intensity, obsessing over the mechanics of desirability as though, if I could get it right, I could finally be the Meg Ryan of my life. A pretty girl who was wanted, desired, beloved. Feminist critic Lauren Berlant would've called it "cruel optimism" and woken me from that white patriarchal spell. Berlant defined cruel optimism as "when something you desire is actually an obstacle to your flourishing . . . when the object that draws your attachment actively impedes the aim that brought you to it."[1] To me, cruel optimism is a welcome package for Black and brown immigrants that offers a road map to success that merely lands them further and further away from it with each step. The kind of optimism that's just as cruel and corny as a pot of gold at the end of the rainbow because in the end, you've been walking for miles before you realize there *is* no "end of the rainbow."

Nevertheless, I persisted. My hands still grasped for this fantasy, regardless of how much I tried to reason with myself. In spicy pursuit of white girlhood, I turned my sights to the women of my residence. Hip, upscale Toronto kids from bougie neighbourhoods like Lawrence Park and Rosedale. Backyards built like parks, backing onto ravines—the smell of pine, and oak, and cedar whooshing through the air, even pavements and quiet roads. Others from small towns, but big fish nonetheless. These girls had summer romances at go-away camps, drunken nights with friends, cottages in the Muskokas. They had sexual

---

1. Lauren Berlant, *Cruel Optimism* (Durham, NC: Duke University Press, 2011), p. 1.

escapades, mediocre grades and a casual belief that even so, everything would be okay.

I traded in my oversized cardigans and jeans for pleather miniskirts in the dead of winter and barely-there tops I promised Yara I would only wear with a tank top underneath. I invested in a pair of brown Ugg boots and a couple of jean miniskirts. I straightened the curls out of my hair every morning. I started on a diet program, where I learned to turn cauliflower into rice and season chicken breast with salt, pepper and oregano. I learned how to do my makeup—how to contour my nose to look thinner, how to line my eyes so they looked larger and more rounded. I was determined to purge the Iranian out of me; my assimilation fantasy depended on it.

A few weeks into the school term, it had become clear to me that sex was the gateway to a relationship. Down the hall was a farm-town beauty with Rapunzel-like brown hair and the brightest-blue eyes I'd ever seen. She'd slept with Junior, a soccer player, and they were dating now. Ruth, my friend from another residence, had slept with Jay, who was now chasing her down for a date. Everyone seemed to want to date Kate, from a few floors up, who had slept with a handful of athletes by the time winter rolled around. No one was courting their love interests, taking them for chaste outings on the weekends. The story always seemed to start with sex.

I set my eyes on Jordan—a big, burly white dude with a bald head, a thick ginger beard and forest-green eyes. A man of few words, if any. I had a theory that men with soft bodies had soft insides. They felt safer to me, though I had absolutely no evidence to back that theory up. Jordan was a rare sighting, though, so I decided I would need to go to him if I was going to make him like me. A few times a week, I made my way down the hall to his apartment and let myself in. People rarely, if ever, locked their doors on campus. A fifteen-minute conversation in his shared living room would ensue, me asking the same questions every time—what are you working on, what are your classes like, what are you reading? Purposefully, I tried to wear my shortest shorts and lowest tops, thinking my boobs were the one thing I had going for me.

One Friday night, I could see people piling into Jordan's place. Music bumping loud, men carrying cases of beer. I sped into my apartment, quickly trying to put together the sexiest look I could: a miniskirt paired with a tank top. Then I popped by one of the other apartments on the floor to see if any of the women were willing to come with me. And after much persuasion, I found one.

By the time we arrived, the place was crowded with tipsy dudes who had already started slurring their words. *You are a hot piece of ass*, I told myself, trying to keep my confidence up. I tried to act cool and collected, keeping my distance from Jordan and occasionally making eye contact. His friends were more touchy-feely than he was, so I gently removed myself from one side of the room and sat near Jordan. At some point, one of the boys reached over and unhooked my bra. Some joke about me being "ready." I laughed along, uncomfortably.

When Jordan wandered into his bedroom to grab something, I followed him. I mustered up as much courage as I could to walk right up to him, grabbed his face and kissed him smack-dab on the lips. Jordan kissed me back and slowly sat down on his bed, pulling me in at the waist. I slowly lowered myself onto his lap. My bra already unhooked, it felt like it was finally happening.

"I've never done this before," I whispered. His fingers immediately stopped at my waist, his face aghast. "You're a virgin?" he asked. "Yeah, you would technically be my first." He immediately lifted me up like a dirty diaper and placed me aside. "No, I can't do this," he said, standing awkwardly by the door. I wasn't sure whether this was an act of compassion or rejection. I walked right out of the apartment and back to my room. No matter how I framed it, it felt embarrassing.

The next week, Julie—who lived on my floor—invited me to her apartment for a hang. She was rarely around because she often went home to visit her boyfriend. But when we found ourselves sharing classes, she reached out.

"Who are you friends with in our building? I never see you!" I told her.

"Mostly Jordan. I see him a lot since we live, like, next to each other. And he's really sweet. So sweet."

Okay, Julie, I thought, *we get it—he's sweet*. Julie talked a lot about Jordan. *A lot*. So much that I started to have questions about whether they really were just friends.

After a brief lull, she finally blurted it out: "He's really into me, but I have a boyfriend." I tried my best not to let the immediate shock, confusion and disappointment I felt show on my face. The more she talked about their connection, the more I held back my tears. Julie had piercing blue eyes, smooth white skin, an edgy haircut, a curvy body. I felt embarrassed to have thought I had a shot with Jordan.

My roommate, Jennifer, was the quintessential image of desirability; if I could have blinked twice and become someone, I would've chosen her. Already a magnet to most of the guys on our campus, within a few weeks she started getting visits from Zip, a senior who lived off-campus. He was intimidatingly tall and muscular, with blue eyes and shoulder-length blond hair. Zip wasn't really into knocking, or hellos, or general pleasantries. He preferred a more thunderous arrival, his gruff voice and booming steps declaring his presence. When he walked through our front door with barely a glance of acknowledgement, I didn't ask questions. When he walked straight into Jennifer's room, I didn't ask questions. And when he opened the bathroom door to Jennifer showering and Jennifer yelped, I didn't ask questions. At least he backed out of the bathroom, I thought.

Zip terrified me, and yet I spoke to no one about it. I had so little experience with boys, I wasn't sure what the norm was, or what was expected. I wasn't sure if his relationship with Jennifer was playful and sweet or awful and unwanted, but I knew it made me uneasy.

One evening, I was sitting in a class where we were discussing experiences of sexism on campus. A young woman raised her hand and started to describe her unsettled feelings about a boy who was aggressively pursuing her roommate. How she feared him, even though it wasn't her that he was pursuing. How she walked slowly and deliberately around her dorm, fearing that any move would set off an emotional grenade. How she smiled, when she wanted to yell, *Get out!*

I could hear the quiver in her voice. "I'm going through the same," I said. As did another woman, and another woman.

News of my comment in that class quickly travelled back to Zip, who promptly came knocking at my door. *BANG, BANG, BANG*—"Open the fucking door!" I opened it to his finger in my face, his chest puffed out, jaw clenched, veins pulsating along his neck. "If you EVER talk about me again, I'll fucking sue you. I'll sue the whole class. I'll sue anyone who talks about me." I stood inches away from that finger, eyes retreating into a squint, shoulders shuddering with each word. *Don't move. Don't fucking move*, I told myself. I dug my soles into the ground until it turned into quicksand and I disappeared myself. He didn't seem to notice that my eyes had retreated into a deer-like blank stare, that my legs had vanished and that I'd floated the fuck away already. When he finally left, I retreated to my room—damp and tired.

Even after the encounter, I felt terror pulsing through my body. I wondered if this was the plague of being an ugly brown girl—death by a thousand cruel remarks, vicious reminders that I was less worthy of dignity than my whiter (read: prettier) counterparts. Cosplaying whiteness wasn't solely about desire; it was about respectability, too. "Ugly" was more than an aesthetic category that determined our level of desirability. Historically, it measured our humanity, often against standards of whiteness. It decided our right to human dignity, our value within a patriarchal society. I was furious at Zip, but I also felt ashamed of myself for not securing his respect; back then, I still felt this lack of respect as a personal failure.

In the winter, I met up with my childhood friend Rana for dinner. Though our families had grown distant after my parents' separation, Rana and I still kept in touch over social media, occasionally checking in on each other. Rana had excelled at university life in ways that gave me hope. She was popular in her program, dating and planning to leave for a semester abroad. She told me she had a belated birthday gift for me, then reached into her wallet and handed me her soon-to-expire driver's licence. "No one will even know this isn't you," she laughed. And it was true: we had strikingly similar features. I tucked it into my wallet immediately, ecstatic to frequent the bars so many others in my residence had been going to with their fake IDs.

At half past ten one Sunday, I pushed onto the dance floor at a local nightclub. One hand loosely holding a vodka-cranberry, the other raised up as my body swayed to Biggie's "Hypnotize." Too drunk to stand, I leaned against the sweaty walls, scanning the room for any eyes that would catch mine.

I locked eyes with Marco, the charming and sweet small-town boy who lived on the fourth floor. Dressed in his regular uniform, red plaid shirt and jeans, he grabbed my waist and pulled me in. "I am so fucking happy to see you," he said, his breath heavy on my neck. I had never felt anything so physically intimate. A stranger pressing their body against mine, sure. The closeness of a boy I knew, his hand on my waist, his breath on me—this was new. It didn't matter that it was Marco, who flirted with most girls, whose "body count" was football player–adjacent, who had just slept with my roommate weeks prior. It didn't matter.

In the quiet of 2 a.m., we stumbled outside onto the main street, the soles of our shoes sticky with alcohol. Marco poked his arm out like a gentleman and I grabbed hold. "Home?" he asked. "Home!" I responded. Barely able to stay standing, barely able to see the pavement in front of me, I relied on his arm to guide me. Twenty minutes later, I found myself lying in Marco's bed, him romancing me with the idea of staying awake all night to watch the sunrise at dawn. On my back, I counted speckles on the ceiling. *One, two, three, four.* Like I was enduring a surgical procedure, I waited for the sex to be done. I watched the speckles on the ceiling move left to right. Right to left. And eventually, I clenched my eyes shut until he finished.

When he did, Marco turned to me and said, "Hey, I'm feeling tired. Let's get you home." There was no more conversation about the sunrise at dawn. In silence, we pulled on some clothes. He popped out his arm again, and I grabbed hold. Stumbling into the hallway, he placed me into the elevator and pushed my floor number. The relief I felt at "getting it over with" was suddenly overshadowed by devastating feelings of shame. I realized he saw me as being good enough for sex, but not for romance, not for a relationship. I felt vile for having had sex, imagining the horror and devastation if my mother were ever to find out. Worst of all, I felt no more desirable or worthy of love than I had before.

Though we were a few floors apart, we never spoke again. We waved in passing sometimes and kept going. I'd wanted to believe that white womanhood could liberate me, deliver me into a world where a brown girl like me could feel wanted. That it could offer girls like Mom and me a chance at human dignity. But it couldn't. Shit, it couldn't even liberate white women.

As for so many other women, it was cruel optimism that kept me grasping at any ounce of attention given to me. It was obvious that the worth we yearned for was not going to be found here. We had to look elsewhere. We had to believe there was an "elsewhere," out beyond culturally prescribed ideas of human value.

9

REVOLUTION

It wasn't until I met Helen, my first-year gender studies professor, that I really started to feel a revolution brewing inside
of me. Meeting Helen was like witnessing a blue moon: an
exceptionally rare occurrence, and one that felt both enchanting and lucky. She was so fully herself, I had nothing and no
one to compare her to. Her short auburn-brown hair, equal
parts parent and punk energy. A scarf draped across her chest,
or sometimes knotted at her neck. Her voice, as soft and gentle
as it was, as tender and kind and affirming as it was, could also
be firm and cutting.

Week after week, Helen would transform the room from
lecture hall to theatre stage. Speaking in monologues, her ver-
bosity radically challenging the brevity of capitalism. Like a
fuck you to corporate culture that abbreviated everything and
anything. Each class felt like a loving eulogy to all those who
had endured the violence of gender-based oppression. To
women like my mother, and her mother, and probably even
her mother's mother. Helen wasn't going to abbreviate any of
it for anybody.

During one of our first lectures, Helen wrote a word on
the chalkboard in capital letters, and I scribbled it so passionately into my notebook that it made the other women in my
row do the same—*P A T R I A R C H Y*. It marked the

beginning of consciously reckoning with the violence and harm that lived in my lineage—stories of those known to me and those not. The concept of patriarchy instantly resonated with me, but it took some time for its meaning, its implications, to unfold.

It was around that time that bell hooks slow-rivered into my thirsty hands the way astrology found queers—a cosmic inevitability. We were reading *Feminism Is for Everybody*, where hooks writes about love in a heterosexist system being about power and domination. That in this context, men were more interested in coercion and control than love and care. I thought about my father, who had abruptly faded from my life. The insidious ways in which he was dominating and controlling. Or how quickly he'd absolved himself from the responsibilities of caring for a child, leaving Mom and Yara to do it all. Every few days, I called Mom, eager to share what I was learning in my gender studies class with Helen. I talked about bell hooks, about her thoughts on power and domination and violence against women. The more we talked, the more it felt like a reversal of roles was happening; I was becoming my mother's teacher and she, my student. Just as I was grappling with what these concepts and ideas meant for me, she was doing the same.

One weekend, I took the Greyhound bus back to Toronto and rode the subway up to Finch Station, where Mom picked me up. "Hi, Rozie!" she squealed joyfully as I got in the car, her arms immediately pulling me in for a hug. She was living in her own apartment now in Richmond Hill, down the street from Yara, who was living with her boyfriend. Yara was still supporting Mom financially, but once I'd left for university, the two decided to find their own spaces. Mom was living in a one-bedroom with a small den that fit a futon, for rare weekends when I came home.

Mom pulled out a container of cubed cantaloupe and waved me over, urging me to eat. She then steeped some chai for the two of us and brought it over to the couches where I was sitting. Both of us placed a sugar cube between our teeth and started sipping our chai. This was the first time Mom had lived completely alone in her life, and her apartment was exactly as I had imagined it would be. A Persian rug under her coffee table, our old bulky brown-leather couches, framed photos of us scattered around. Above all, it was meticulously clean and organized. There was something that felt lighter about her, too. More joy in her than during those years in the basement, where most of our light came from the dreaded fluorescent lighting.

When she asked me about my studies, I launched into a monologue about the devastating stories of domestic violence I had heard from Helen, and all the reasons why women stay in those situations. Her face looked pensive. "What are you thinking about?" I asked her. "You know—the day of your birth was the day your father changed," she replied, her tone implying the ache of an old wound. She drew in a deep breath and recounted the harrowing ways my father had physically abused her during their marriage. Though Yara and Yasaman witnessed it as children, it was something she had never shared with anyone. Nor had my sisters ever shared it with me.

Not knowing how to talk about it with her family, she found ways to keep herself as safe as she could. Learned how far out of line she could go before the threat of a hammering hand arose. Or to say yes, unequivocally, when guests were around. She even got her hair cut into a pixie because it made it difficult to grab and pull. I winced, trying to stop visualizing the violence.

Her voice quieted as she recounted how, one day, she waddled into her ESL class with a bruised eye. "I was pregnant with you and none of the makeup would cover the bruise, even with everything I tried," she explained, exasperation in her voice. Her teacher, fixing upon her face with a worried gaze, came over to her and asked her what had happened. "I told her I fell off a bike," she said. "We were so scared back then. What would we do if they sent us back, or worse, took our kids from us?"

At the end of the class, her teacher pulled her aside, pleading with her to share the truth about her eye. But even with all her pleas, Mom remained tight-lipped. So, instead, she leaned over to Mom and whispered: "If a man is coming at you, you pick up the phone and say you're dialling 9-1-1. Tell him that. Okay?" Mom nodded, and returned home.

Flashing forward, Mom recalled the day after my birth, when my father invited his friends over and instructed her to cook dinner for them. I could hear his voice saying it, too. His nonchalance, and how immovable he was when he decided on something.

"I was so tired," she explained to me, dragging the *so* to emphasize her exhaustion. "I know, Mom, I can imagine," I reassured her. Upon saying no, she caught a glimpse of Baba's hand folding into a fist again, and she rushed to the phone. "I picked it up," she said as she picked up an imaginary phone, "and I said, 'I call 9-1-1.' He never did it again." The firmness in her voice revealed a sense of pride. "Good for you, Mom," I said, wanting her to hear the pride in my voice, too.

Though Mom held on to that story as the day my father changed, I came to think of it more as a story about my mother than my father. Her standing in her power, her agency again. And I thought about how significant it must have been for my mother, who had armoured herself in secrecy for so long, to have another person not only witness her wounding, but want to protect her, too. "I really liked that teacher . . . she was so nice to me." Mom smiled pensively, her eyes glassy. "Me too," I said to her, grateful to the woman who, unknowingly, opened the cage door for my mother and reminded her she could fly. I thought, *I wish she could've seen her fly*.

In the days that followed, I felt heartache more than anything. Like I had looked directly into the sun and now was seeing flashes of the violence everywhere. I was beginning to see that there were secrets my mother and sisters shouldered together, never speaking them aloud. That the protectiveness that bonded my sisters and my mother together had come—at least in part—from knowing violence so intimately. I was shouldering this secret, too, now. And with that came a swiftly emerging protectiveness.

When the academic year was over, my mother and Khaleh Sima helped me move into a four-bedroom apartment five minutes from the university, where I'd be living with three other women. The two had volunteered to help me pack my room into boxes. Mostly, folding away my clothes and dumping my books into a big bin. As I said goodbye to my bedroom in my on-campus apartment and prepared to walk out, my mother remembered that we hadn't cleaned out the desk drawers yet. She opened up a drawer and gasped at the sight of piles and piles of condoms, to which Khaleh Sima also gasped—both of them looking to me for answers. I tried to keep my cool, promptly explaining that they weren't *really* mine and that the residence staff gave them to us, even if we didn't want them, as part of sexual health education. A half truth. I shoved handfuls of condoms into the garbage bin with a frazzled smile as they watched and talked about how ridiculous it was that the school pushed condoms on their students.

Moving from a student residence to an off-campus apartment felt like I was moving deeper into adulthood and all the questions that came with it. Mostly existential questions, about who I wanted to be. I had decided to change my major from communication studies to gender studies. That and English literature—because you couldn't take gender studies alone, and of the options, I could most get behind reading fiction for the next three years.

A few weeks after my move, the excitement I felt dissolved into fear and anxiety. A string of sexual assaults had started happening, right outside my building and across my neighbourhood. It horrified me to know that, from my ground-floor window, I'd heard nothing. That something like that could happen so quietly I could sleep through it all. I felt lucky to have missed it, and guilty for thinking that way. I started ruminating constantly on why it had happened to those women, and not me. I had heard stories of people being protected from danger by the spirits of their loved ones. Perhaps my departed ancestors stood alongside me, their hands in mine, walking me to safety. Or maybe it was Mom's prayers really working. I wanted to know why *I* had been lucky, and not them. Actually, I wanted it not to be luck at all. I wanted something more than the flimsy weight of chance, or the cosmos, or faith. I wanted something with teeth, something made of metal.

Knowing the threat of violence in my neighbourhood, I took things into my own hands and developed my own system of self-protection. Never leave home without keys between your fingers. Don't wear anything too loud—literally—nothing that jingle-jangles or click-clacks. Yell *Fire*, not *Help*. Look around, obsessively, and if someone wants to approach you, run. Directions? Run. "Can I ask you something?" Run. There were no exceptions to the system.

Helen's office hour had become my weekly refuge. Reliably, I could cry there and know that I was allowed to. That there was space for that kind of emotional vulnerability. Some weeks, Helen just sat with me as I cried, witnessing my pain and offering a tissue. Others, she would take a deep breath and say, "So, Roza—what do we do about all of this?" referring to the magnitude of violence women were experiencing on campus, in their homes, in their workplaces, everywhere.

I decided to volunteer at the local sexual violence centre and enlisted for months-long training to get on their support team. The decision was one part a response to Helen's question and one part the desire to find community with feminists— who now, to me, were emblematic of the safety I craved and the protectiveness I yearned to embody. The training was a two-hour class in the evenings on the second floor of a dilapidated building in Kitchener, white paint peeling from its bricks. In the daylight, Kitchener was a beautifully quaint town with heritage buildings, corner coffee shops and NGOs. At night, it was eerily quiet.

At the first class I met Ace, a volunteer and co-facilitator with the centre. I was immediately drawn to them. Short brown hair, inked arms, hairy legs, a backpack covered in pins that read "Fuck the Patriarchy," "Queer as in 'fuck you'" and "No to rape culture." Ace ignited a buzzing in my belly that inched me closer and closer to them. When they asked me how I was, I nervously tucked my hair behind my ears. When their mouth opened, I traced their lips with my eyes. Eventually, I started to daydream about what it would feel like to kiss them. Somehow, the thought still hadn't crossed my mind that I was queer. To me, these were the innocent thoughts that everyone had at this age, when we were all discovering ourselves.

The other trainees were of different ages and backgrounds. Older retired women who wanted to give back to the community, young folks who I had seen in passing at the university, queer people invested in activism. On Thursday nights we sat around in a circle and talked about things I was newly learning about and giving language to—rape culture, suicide, gender-based violence as a whole. Their passion, their rage, their empathy ignited the same in me. Here, I wasn't chasing an idea of who I needed to be. I was discovering who *I* was and who I wanted to be: someone who was fiercely protective of all those hurt by the violence of patriarchy.

A couple weeks into the training, Mom came to visit me. We drove to a nearby Iranian restaurant because I was desperately craving Persian food. Between bites of kabob, I enthusiastically told her about my new volunteering gig and the conversations we were having. I motored on about involving myself in feminist community organizing, like joining the Centre for Women and Trans People on campus or volunteering at marches. At some point, I noticed Mom's silence. I could see the hesitation in her face. "What is it?" I asked her, immediately frustrated. She took a deep breath and said, "Don't go too far into this stuff. You know? Focus on school. Don't go too much into feminism and those things." Her tune had changed so quickly from our previous conversations, where it felt like she was learning and revealing so much about herself. "I *am* going to go too much into these things, because it's important," I shot back at her. "Focus on your school," she reiterated. Irritated, I ate silently for the rest of our dinner, as did she. I couldn't understand why she couldn't just be supportive.

When I first started talking to my mother about my gender studies class, she had proudly claimed she was a feminist during her teens and early-adult years. I wouldn't have questioned this statement except for the strange disagreements we were having about my new involvement in feminist circles. I had returned home for the winter break and was working on a project related to Muslim women's religious right to wear a hijab. The two of us were sitting on the couch when the news started talking about a potential ban on the niqab in Montreal. "Isn't that ridiculous, Mom?" I turned to her, feeling certain she would affirm the ridiculousness of the bill. To my surprise, my mother was unfazed by it, claiming she could understand it. "Well, when you live in another country, you have to live by *their* rules," she explained. My eyes widened, horrified by the sentiment. "Mom, how can you be a feminist if you don't believe that *all* women have right to decide what they wear?" I asked. No matter how I framed it, Mom was resolute that she was allowed to have her own opinions, and that was how she felt about the matter.

I wanted to understand how we'd gotten from point A to point B. Mom the feminist, the gender-equity advocate, to Mom who thought it was okay to have a niqab ban. Or at least, that it wasn't *so* terrible. So I asked her about the 1979 Revolution back home, trying to piece together who she was then.

Mom emphasized that her involvement was because of her brother Shahin. She beamed, just remembering him. Her stories sketched out an intriguing image: a man who debated ferociously about capitalism, justice and collective liberation, arguing the merits of communism versus socialist systems of power with anyone and everyone who would listen. In awe of the civil rights movement, he would reflect fondly on Martin Luther King Jr. and Malcolm X—their stories deepening his belief in the power of people and movement-building. He dreamed of a government that served the working class, instead of catering to the rich as he felt the Shah did. And he believed that a Muslim democracy would lead us there.

Mom recalled being eighteen and eager to sponge up all of Shahin's wisdom. He would walk her to a barely-there building—just four erect walls, no ceiling and no lights—where activists would make their protest signs. Her eyes lit up with a familiar glimmer as she recalled him telling her how they quietly delivered the signs in the dark of night, from one house to another, even inviting her along some nights. Or how he taught her how to make a fist in the air, like the fist he had seen in pictures of the Black Power movement. She recollected the many nights of protest when the whole family would join him, lining the streets with their signs.

Admittedly, it was hard to imagine my mother throwing up a fist or chanting protest anthems. Perhaps what was most challenging was understanding how a woman who was once so committed to mobilization and change could become so apolitical. The more I learned about her revolutionary years, the more I hungered for more stories. I was chasing an old version of her, not wanting to stop until I found her.

Over that year, I continued to dig into our histories, wanting Mom to tell me what had happened in 1979. I wanted to understand how she—or perhaps more aptly, our whole family—could suddenly abandon the more radical versions of themselves.

"Mom, if you were a feminist, then how could you want that man to run the country?" I asked, referring to Ayatollah Khomeini. His leadership had led to a devastating war on women's rights.

The question exasperated her. She responded that she had heard only vague rumblings about Khomeini. Since he'd been living in exile in France, she never considered that he would return and become their next leader. She emphasized that while there was unity in their collective desire for more freedom, there were differences in the kind of leadership and society people imagined and wanted. She aligned with the leftists who called for a Muslim democracy, where leadership was selected through an electoral process. I was learning that the desire for a Muslim democracy was *not* to be confused with a desire for Khomeini's leadership.

"What about Dayee Shahin?" I asked her. I wondered if it was wrong to ask her to keep remembering something that so obviously pained her. Was I no different than the archeologists who dug up sacred burial grounds for museum artifacts? I reminded myself that it was my history, too, and I deserved to know it. She lamented about how Dayee Shahin spiralled after Ayatollah Khomeini came into power, fiercely adamant that this regime would not deliver the kind of liberation he sought. He continued to write letters, to organize, to fight. "Someone said he pushed through a crowd of people one time at an airport where Khomeini was leaving for a flight and handed him his letter, telling him everything he disagreed with," she explained. "That's what they said."

In ways, Mom struggled to remember the exact truth— unsure of what she had witnessed herself and what was told to her by others. There was Dayee Shahin, the boy she adored and sneaked sips of liquor with at family parties; there was the activist and friend she admired; and there was the bigger perception of him as a revolutionary, a family story that transcended their relationship.

As Dayee Shahin's opposition to the regime grew, members of the regime clamoured to find him and arrest him. Mom looked at me and said, "You know what happened." I stared at her, wanting her to keep going, to say it out loud again. She continued, recounting the day when, after Shahin was missing for hours, he showed up at their parents' home in disarray. He had been arrested for treason and, in the regime's usual cruel manner, he had been walked across a bridge and thrown into a body of water, left for dead. To survive, he had hidden under the bridge until it was dark enough to walk home.

Less than a year following the revolution, he fell into a dark depression that made him nearly unrecognizable to mom. Once full of hope, he now languished in the dread and misery of what he saw as a failed revolution. He turned to heroin to ease the pain. Mom remembered the brief moments when he would surface again, promising he was getting sober this time. "He tried, he really tried," she pleaded as if trying to convince me. But inevitably, his pain and anguish would become too overwhelming to bear, and he would isolate and self-medicate again. It wasn't until the mid '80s that he finally found his way out of the grips of depression and addiction, and on the path of recovery. Soon after, Dayee Shahin disappeared again. This time, the last. After days of the family frantically searching for him, a stranger came across his body in a carefully landscaped park.

The stranger who found him had witnessed an officer laying a blanket over his torso in the early morning. Hours later, the man noticed he was still there, unmoving. The sun was still kissing his face—a delicate glow that offered the illusion of life, as if he was still taking in the small joys of this world. "*Yadesh bekhair*," my mother said with a sigh, as if her brother was still in the room. "It wasn't right for you to leave this world like this." I paused my questions after seeing tears welling up in her eyes. I felt like I had pushed my mother too far with all the remembering.

Not all of this was new information. On some days, Mom would sip her chai through a sugar cube, place the glass teacup back down on the plate and say, "They killed him. They did this." They, referencing the regime. Or she would be flipping channels, cutting through static to find one that actually worked, and say it was the heroin that killed him. Or she would simply say that the world hadn't been ready for him—that he was ahead of his time. By the time I was in my teens, she had stopped uttering his name almost entirely, but her aches never quieted.

I tried not to ask questions about the past anymore, even though I wondered about her days waiting for Shahin following his disappearance. She never told me about them, as if there was life and then there was death. Nothing in between. Almost as if she preferred skipping the record forward for herself at different moments in the story—a willed amnesia. Maybe forgetting was a kind of rest for my mother from all the aching. And after everything I had learned about my father and her, she deserved that rest. However complicated our own relationship was in the moment.

Mom continued driving up to Waterloo with bags and bags of food for me. Three containers of *aash*, two for the freezer. Two containers of *gheimeh*, both for the freezer. Groceries from the Persian store—pita bread, feta, chicken, a bag of rice. Instead of talking about my growing interest in organizing, I continued talking about feminism theoretically, somewhat detached from the concepts. Sometimes, we just talked about food. Like how many times you had to run water over rice before you cooked it, or what *advieh*, a collection of spices, really was. What she didn't know couldn't hurt her, I thought.

Yet I could sense that *she* could sense what I wasn't saying—that I wasn't going to stop. Sometimes, I caught her staring at me, her eyes full of concern. Perhaps it was hard for her to look at me now without feeling the fears she'd probably felt during and after the Revolution. The ones she'd felt when she looked at Dayee Shahin back then, and maybe even herself. I sensed the tug-of-war in her. Part of her wanting to kill the spirit of revolution and resistance in me, before it killed me. An act of compassion for my own good. And the other part of her wanting to see me freer than she herself had ever been.

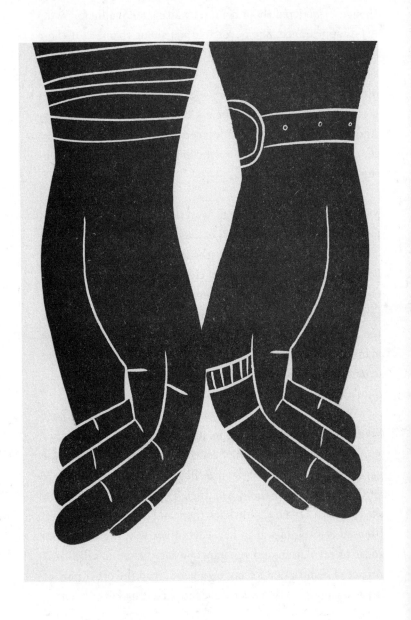

10

LOVE

In my third year, the gender studies department had packed up its offices and moved to a building on the edge of campus. If you wanted to visit your professors, you'd have to cross the street from the main campus and walk into a building that mostly housed a lineup of nail-biting students waiting for their student loan cheques. Oh, and the archeology students, who, much like us, were regarded as a relic of the past.

Helen's office had continued to be my weekly refuge. During one of my visits, coffee in hand, I waved hello to the office administrator and turned the corner to a hallway lined with other students. Some who saw Helen's office as I saw it, a refuge; others wanting structure and guidance for her loosely led assignments. Their huffs and puffs could tell you who was who. I placed my backpack on the floor, sitting next to a slender person with bleach-blond hair, a torn black shirt and tattoos up their arm. They sat with their head hanging low—a head so low it begged for a generous hand to swoop beneath it and carry its weight. And though my polite upbringing yelled, "Ask what they need!" something in me turned away. When it was their turn, the door opened and Helen's gentle eyes invited them in. They slowly stood and entered the office. A few moments later, Helen opened the door and said: "Roza, can you get them water?" I walked over to the water cooler, poured a cup of water, and handed it in to Helen. I lingered only momentarily to see them collapsed in their chair, eyes darting away.

I saw them again in my fourth year, when they arrived late to a gender studies class. Their quiet steps followed by the thump of their backpack touching ground, the *zip-zip* of it opening, the crunch of hands in search of a pen amid a proliferation of paper. In hindsight, they looked like the unofficial third member of Tegan and Sara. Short, messy hair, skinny jeans and big hipster glasses. Their body so thin it glided delicately across the room, sliding into a desk in the front row with ease. Their face pierced with silver jewellery: one ring on the eyebrow, one at the septum. They radiated cool, don't-give-a-fuck energy.

I was all give-a-fuck. Before arriving to class, I spent an hour each morning attaching long brown hair extensions into my scalp, brushing them together, straightening them from the top, and waving them at the bottoms. I painted my face with golden-brown foundation, delicately blushed, bronzed and contoured it to look thinner, and extended my eyes upward. I cared, deeply. While I'd found my feminist crew at the Centre for Women and Trans People, I still valued and hung out with the friends I had acquired early on. Fun-loving straight women with whom I drunkenly gallivanted about town 'til the early hours of the morning. I was conscious of but not immune to the beauty ideals we all strived for.

When I'd arrived ten minutes early to class that day, I'd found a spot at the front near my friends, and more importantly, near the professor. I'd wiggled myself into the seat quietly and gently, until the table invited my body in.

When Ren arrived, my sunflower eyes wandered west towards them, my body elongating, tilting and swaying in their direction. Noticing their tapping legs, their slouched shoulders, their soft, darting gaze. I tried to locate them within my carefully constructed maps of whiteness. Fingers moved gently, curiously, along the map, moving across mountainous terrains and white sandy islands, up and down coasts and across grand cities; there was nothing like Ren. I was looking at a map in search of a sun.

In the weeks that followed, just before the lecture began, I followed them to the right side of the room, planting myself into the seat directly behind them. I mused at the tattoo on the back of their arm, a black-ink script that read *love yourself*. Maybe it was the magnetic charm of their awkward mannerisms, their dorky grin when I asked them their name, or the way they looked down immediately when they offered a brilliant thought. Maybe it was that, beneath the hard exterior of piercings and tattoos, I could sense something soft and tender. Maybe it was that they felt wild in ways I had never given myself permission to be.

"We've met before," Ren said, with an inviting smile. "Really?" I asked, pretending not to remember. "Yeah, at Helen's office. You brought me water."

One day, when class was over, Ren and I migrated back to the main campus, making our way to the Centre. The Centre was a small, quaint space: yellow walls, two comfy couches, one computer, a small feminist library in the back, a collection of contraceptives and menstrual products, *Bitch* magazine. More conservative folks on campus, which was most of campus, deemed us man-haters, which felt deeply offensive given that we "man-haters" were not a monolith. There were pretty-girl feminists, hairy-leg-fuck-your-gender-norms feminists, straight feminists and queer feminists, fuck-the-patriarchy-but-capitalism-is-kinda-okay feminists, baby feminists, anarchist feminists, white feminists (also known as we're-all-sisters-here feminists) and even a few feminists who were men.

Ren sat down on the couch, and I placed myself directly beside them, both of us grinning like teenage sweethearts. My mind had yet to catch up to my swooning body, gleefully lighting up as our arms brushed against each other. "I wanna see photos of you from high school," I said, a thinly veiled beg for more time on the couch, more time near them. Ren opened up their laptop, flipping from one photo to another, from one story to the next of who they were in high school, their hair decisions, their softball days.

Eventually, sitting on that couch with Ren, the words wound down to a slow quiet, leaving nothing else but to part ways. And in my desperation to keep us connected, the words fell out of my mouth before my head had time to fact-check them. "A bunch of us are going to Starlight on Friday. You should come," I said, perplexed by my own invitation. The following couple days were spent orchestrating these imaginary plans, desperately finding a gang of feminists willing to brave the white neoliberal dance floors of small-town Ontario.

In the hush-hush of my room, I lay on my back, listening to Ani DiFranco against the buzzing in my belly, quickly solidifying into steel knots. *What the hell are you doing?* I thought, dumbfounded by the events that I, myself, had set into motion. I had never thought I was queer. Most of my crushes had been on boys and men. The experiences with Ace, the year before, and Shireen, during middle school, were never clearly legible to me as "crushes." I had repressed both, refusing to acknowledge either as attraction or desire.

In most queer stories I knew of, there would be more to it than a simple falling into queerness, of a curiosity followed. There would be the dramatic realization of my queerness in my younger years, and the subsequent sense of otherness. I would tell you stories of how it felt to be the "queer one" surrounded by straight people in high school. I would describe the agony of being "in the closet," of not being able to come out to my immigrant mother. There would be the teen angst, and rebellion, and repression. And there would be signs, which I'd reflect on fondly, with laughter—like *aha, I should've known*. Like playing softball, or starting a gay-straight alliance at school.

But there wasn't much more backstory to this. That's the thing about queerness. For some of us, our arrival into queerness doesn't begin with agony and otherness. It begins with quiet tenderness—so quiet, you might miss it if you're not paying attention.

I felt unprepared to "do" queerness, and an invisible hand seemed to reach out to my shoulders and pull me upright, square to a blank Google tab. I let my fingers lead.

Google: queer people, sex

Google: queer women, sex

Google: what is scissoring

Society's hyper-sexual ideas about queerness had caught up to me, naturally launching me into the only starting point I could come to: a study on the mechanics of queer sex. Intellectualization is a masterful way of avoiding the uncomfortable. There was no googling of tender coming-out stories, of what queerness actually is, of how to tell your friends and family. No. Blush-faced and still, I watched lesbian porn so clearly made for the male gaze, my body gagged. It recoiled, tightened and damn near flung me across the room. *Is this what sex is supposed to look like?* I wondered.

There was something taboo about it—seeing women supposedly experiencing pleasure. When I was eight, I'd learned that if you sat on your feet the "right way," you could feel something akin to pleasure. I would wiggle my toes and curiously explore the tingling, unaware of what it was.

Sitting amongst the kids at a *mehmooni* (dinner party), I'd sat cross-legged, tucking my foot into my vulva. Stern-eyed, my mother had walked over and whispered: "*Eibeh*." She untucked my foot and walked away, watching me from the other side of the room to be sure I wouldn't return it. And it was probably then that I'd last felt pleasure around my own body.

"*Eib*" is an Arabic word used amongst Iranians to denote shameful behaviour. It was Mom's go-to phrase for anything outside or vaguely pushing the bounds of Muslim body norms. Girls sitting wide-legged was eib. A shirt too short was eib. A skirt too short was eib. Vulvas and breasts were most certainly eib. By the beginning of my early adolescence, I understood that almost anything to do with my body and with pleasure was shameful, and something to be avoided entirely.

Even as I watched lesbian porn in the quiet of my room, I could feel my face turn peach-red, and hear a faint whisper—*eib*.

I woke to the sun peering in through the bedroom window the morning after the club with Ren, and felt the heat of our bodies enmeshed. I folded myself towards them, noticing the stark contrast of their porcelain-white skin against my brown body, their small, delicate hands. "I've never done this before," I said. "That, this . . . all of it." "Really? I wouldn't have known," Ren said, their eyes gazing into mine, a gentle twinkle like sun kissing water. My hands walked over to their arms, tracing black ink and blue veins. We stayed there for what felt like an hour, gripping hands in the stillness. This was a new kind of intimacy. The few people I'd had sex with had left before sunrise, promising to text me and never following through.

"Do you . . . wannaaaa . . . get . . . breakfasttttttt?" I said, stretching the words out like taffy. We decided on Angel's diner and walked in holding hands. A general mix of white folks populated the dated diner—young college students and retirees taking their grandkids for Sunday breakfast. We slotted ourselves into a quiet booth in a corner. Beige leather squeaked beneath our legs as we wiggled our way towards each other from across the wide wooden table.

Against the humdrum shades of mahogany-red and beige-brown in the diner, Ren stood out. Their short hair, piercings and tattoos loud emblems of queerness in a town deeply invested in white, cis-hetero, middle-class respectability. It felt unnerving to be so visible with them.

Brown girls like me come from lineages of quieted women who learned silence as a tool for survival. We watched our mothers bite their tongues to keep quiet until there was no tongue left. We watched them make themselves small until they nearly disappeared, and we, the daughters of these alchemists, learned how to blend in. We learned how to "do" whiteness enough to keep us mild, palatable. Queerness was the antithesis of what it meant to be palatable.

I was both enamoured by how deliciously punk Ren was and fearful of them. The more their body leaned forward, the more I sensed the leviathan rising in my belly, its tentacle arms thrashing in rapid waters, a gurgling storm that violently whooshed against the confines of skin and bone. Ren's half-moon eyes stared at me from across the table, inspecting my face for signs of requited desire.

When their hands found their way atop mine on the table, the sickness in my belly roared louder. I didn't know it then, but I was fighting a panic attack. Ren's voice sounded muffled, and the clinking and clanging of spoons against coffee mugs felt sharply amplified. I was doing my best to even my breath, to keep the nausea at bay.

We finished eating, paid and left. And when we unwound our hands from each other and walked separate paths home, I felt like I could breathe again.

In my bedroom, I puzzled over the feelings of disgust, of nausea, wondering if they were signs I wasn't queer after all.

One of my professors assigned us Julia Kristeva's *Black Sun* for class reading, lauding it as essential feminist theory that would signficantly change us. I walked my regular route from Regina Street to the Centre, where I gently plopped my bag on the ground, folded my legs up on the couch and opened up my readings. I understood very little, at first. The density of Kristeva's text taunted me, an opacity I wasn't used to. I was initially unchanged, but eager to understand more.

I became an avid reader of Julia Kristeva, intrigued by her relentless curiosity about the darker edges of human existence. Bloodied bodies, rotten corpses, yellow pus, the dirt under our fingernails, the shit we rarely language. Kristeva spoke emphatically of the abject, this horrifying thing that we were both deliciously drawn to and seemingly disgusted by. The things that we both desired and rejected. I was fascinated by this place of *both/and*, where craving and disgust co-existed.

Disgust, in Kristeva's work, is something that operates as a survival mechanism, protecting us from illness. In the case of food, repulsion and vomiting act as protective, turning us away from rotting, spoiled, contaminated foods. Disgust was about more than food, though; it was about social ideas of moral goodness, purity and acceptability. For Kristeva, what we are pulled towards and disgusted or horrified by is emblematic of the parts of ourselves we have repressed to maintain order—within our identities, our selfhoods, our societies. Disgust becomes an internal mechanism that turns us away from what is deemed morally "bad," away from transgressing social and cultural norms.

Suddenly, the urge to vomit, the nausea, weren't so puzzling anymore. I wondered about whether the disgust I was feeling was less about Ren and I, and more about societal and cultural ideas about queerness. Perhaps I had subconsciously internalized queerness as morally *bad*. There was no overt rejection of queerness in my family. But no one spoke much of it, either. Sometimes, what's not spoken about is just as telling as what is.

And then there was what happened outside the home. In middle school, boys never failed to hurl "fag" at each other like an insult—and the response: immediate defensiveness. "That's so gay" referenced anything you hated during my high school years. And one of my peers in high school left, only to return months later to tell the story of how fearful he'd been to be queer and out at the school.

Now, just as I felt intrigued and pulled towards queerness, I felt terrified and repulsed, too. I didn't know how to reconcile my connection with and desire for Ren with the intense fear I felt about what it meant to be queer; I was a person who had always sought safety, and queerness left me feeling exposed and unprotected. I had learned to armour myself, to keep myself safe by blending in, conforming, aligning, being good. In ways, it felt like queerness was demanding a dis-armouring that felt both deeply vulnerable and unsafe. Both of my hands gripped at the protection I had built up over my childhood and teen years, fearful of what would happen if I let go of any of it. And while I wasn't sure I was ready for that yet, I also knew I couldn't ignore the feelings I had for Ren.

ELSEWHERE

If I'm honest, I didn't know how to be romantic. Erotic novels and romantic comedies existed in a fantastical dimension, and there wasn't much to learn from my parents' marriage, at least along the lines of intimacy. I still wondered whether there was more to the relationship between them than what I could see—perhaps a quiet closeness or past romance. After their separation, I asked Mom how they'd got engaged. "I didn't want to marry him—I wanted to study," she explained. "Then why did you marry him?" I asked her, genuinely curious.

I'd known that my father's family had known my mother's family for years. My father's dad was a military man who was often moving around for work. During the summers, he would leave the kids at Baba Ali's house and pick them up when school was to begin again. As my father grew up, he became a favourite in my mother's family. Always showing up to help her parents—from something in the house breaking down to car rides for appointments. Eventually, my maternal grandparents came to see him as a beloved son.

Though my mother and father were childhood friends, she wasn't interested in anything more than that. She pined for a boy in her neighbourhood who reciprocated her affections. As teens, she and the boy had brief conversations here and there, stolen glances as they walked home from school.

Eventually, the two planned that they would both go off to university one day, and after getting their degrees, they would marry each other.

That was Mom's plan until my father set his sights on her, relentlessly vying for her hand in marriage. He tried everything in the book to get Mom's attention. He drove to her school, waiting until the bell rang to drive her home. When she said no and promptly boarded her regular bus, he followed the bus until it dropped her off close to home, where he would drive alongside as she walked, pleading for her hand in marriage. He spoke to her parents, making the argument that he was a suitable choice as her husband. He waited for her in her home, and even when she kicked him out, yelling, "No, no, no," he still came back. And when she finally got into his car, one day after school, and explained that she had plans to continue with her education, making it clear she didn't want to get married yet, he still turned up at her home, begging.

Eventually, her parents demanded that Mom marry him, refusing to let her put off marriage to go to university, or to marry the boy in the neighbourhood with an uncertain financial future. After countless attempts to change their minds, she complied, because it was her only option. She knew that she could either comply or be exiled from the family. Her story simply confirmed what I had already known—that my parents' relationship was one of duty, not desire. At least for Mom.

What I wanted with Ren was a different kind of connection, and intimacy, and romance—even if there were parts of me that still recoiled, terrified of our relationship. A couple weeks into dating, we had settled into tender rituals that dispelled my fears so that I felt nothing but warmth and affection. In the evenings, we would tuck away at the Centre and lie on the couches. Between lively conversations about who we would be as cyborgs and Judith Butler's ideas on gender performativity, we read feminist and queer literature. I would glance over at them, calmed by their green eyes tracing the words on their page. Or wanting to nuzzle my nose against their nose, and press my lips to theirs. There was heat just being near them, like in all the steamy romances I had grown up reading.

Then we would walk ten minutes up the street to my apartment and collapse in bed under a pile of blankets. Ren had introduced me to *The L Word*, a show that followed a group of queer women—their friendships, their messy romances, their fuck-ups. At half past ten, my eyes would be glued to the screen, consuming the series as if it was a documentary. Though I could define what queerness was, I struggled to envision what it meant to embrace a queer life in full view of the people I had spent my life trying not to offend. To *be queer* felt possible, like it was a matter of identity, of what was within, something I could quietly acknowledge. To *live queer* felt like the antithesis of much of my being. It was a matter of self-discovery, however complicated that process was, however painful it became. And perhaps more terrifying, alignment with that self, sometimes at the expense of belonging, or the simple comfort of moving through the world unnoticed. It was what Ren was good at. Knowing themself deeply beyond the bounds of normativity, and perpetually aligning with that self—in values, in politics, in practices and even in aesthetics. It was a messy process for them, and I was learning that it was messy for all of us.

The show, in its messiness, was also easing me into this reality. Considering the critiques I now know of its hypersexualization of queer women and mishandling of a trans character's plot, it feels odd to say this—but back then, it offered me a road map. Carmen, in particular. A femme, queer woman of colour played by Sarah Shahi, who in real life was a mixed-race

Iranian Spanish woman. My eyes lit up when she came onscreen. In her face, I could see myself. I remember a particular scene where she wakes up and describes a dream to her love interest, Shane, in which Shane gives another woman a sacred tattoo that both of them have. For the rest of the morning, Carmen is devastated by what happened in the dream. As strange and silly as that was, it was something I could see myself feeling upset by. A moment of *Ah, there I am*. And eventually these small moments of seeing myself accumulated to the point where I could start imagining living a queer life.

While our affection for each other seemed tender and ever-blooming indoors, it felt cold and confusing outside my bedroom or the Centre. There were many painful moments where Ren would reach for my hand and I would pull away. Or I would turn to Ren and whisper, "Everyone is looking at you," as I cowered, wanting to disappear. Eventually, I decided to merge my two worlds—the inside and outside, my straight friends from first year and my current circle of feminist friends. I ripped off the Band-Aid on a Saturday night, when I knew my straight friends would be going out. Sent them a message that went something like this: *Can I bring my partner? Also, I'm queer*. Their response seemed neither positive or negative as they welcomed Ren to join, with a few questions about when this had all happened.

That Saturday night, we decided to go to Gem, our usual Friday spot for hip-hop night, where the crowd was mostly folks of colour who loved to bump and grind to Biggie Smalls and 112. On Saturdays, they played EDM and the crowd was mostly white, straight and very drunk. It was rare for me to go. Ren arrived at my house early in their club-ready attire: a cut-out shirt with wide openings on the sides, acid-washed pants and a face full of piercings. *They look too gay*, I thought, starting to feel sweaty and nervous about the whole thing. My stomach rumbling with regret. Truthfully, when we were at the Centre or in our gender studies classes, I swooned over Ren, finding it very punk that they had their own style. It was cool, and rebellious, and radical. But in a crowd of straight people, and at a club no less, I felt the opposite. I wore the most normatively feminine outfit I could, trying to temper Ren's—a black miniskirt, a see-through tank top, and a belt.

The two of us walked down the dark stairs of Gem as the security eyed Ren. I rushed towards my friends, who were clustered together on the dance floor, swaying in the sweaty crowd. I briefly introduced Ren and tried to pretend everything was normal, when in fact, it felt very *not* normal. Perhaps it was my own distress that made me distrustful of my friends, too. I thought they were staring at me, trying to piece together how I'd suddenly "become" queer, and I spiralled internally, wondering if it *was* all a lie. Ren, smiling widely and dancing with them, tried to grab my hand, to which I stepped back and pulled away. Smiled, to keep up the illusion of *everything is fine*, but I knew they knew. The gaze of anyone from the crowd felt hot on my body, scorching me with what I perceived as judgment.

Eventually, Ren had one too many drinks and spilled one on the already sticky floor. It wasn't unusual for people to spill their drinks—the space was crowded, and the only way to move was to bump against others, to push and push. The security guard immediately yanked Ren out of the crowd and dragged them up the stairs and out the door. *This is homophobia!* Ren yelled on the way out. I followed them, waving at my friends with a heavy dose of shame. I knew Ren was right. The only people I had seen kicked out of the club were belligerently drunk people, and Ren wasn't that. But still, walking home that night, I wished we hadn't gone at all.

This new life felt so vastly different from my carefully crafted, non-disruptive identity. I was learning that to live queer meant being willing to unsettle the norm, to disrupt it. That people would stare—not out of desire, but out of rejection, disgust and even hatred. That the double takes, the burning stares were signs that you were doing it right. And truthfully, I wondered if I had the courage and grit to live this life. Ren clearly did. And on nights when it was just the two of us, lying in my bed and holding each other's faces, I wanted to, desperately.

I decided to come out to Yara during fall reading week, when I was staying with her and her husband. They were going to be travelling during the latter part of the week, so it would give her time to process it. Ren and I had been dating for over a month, and this felt like the next step in integrating my worlds. I'd spent three days trying to figure out who I would come out to first, mapping out my family in order of who would be most receptive. Yara was the natural first choice. She was the most liberal, having grown up here. Mom was a wild card when it came to her opinions, so I thought she could be second. Yasaman was now Christian and more conservative, so she would be last. Or my father would come last, if ever at all.

I had rehearsed what I would say, repeated the script in the mirror until I no longer stumbled over the word *queer*. The script was: *Yara, I'm queer. I've been dating Ren for a month and felt it was time for you to know.* I didn't know when I was going to do it. Every time I tried, I felt sick. The room would start swirling and my body would shake. One day, Yara was standing at the door of her garage, waiting for her dogs to poop outside. I thought, *It's now or never*, especially because they were leaving soon. My chest and throat felt constricted as I walked over to her, a blank stare across my face. Now, breathing heavily, the words erupted out of me like hot lava.

"Yara . . . I have to tell you something . . . I'm queer, and I have a partner," I blurted out. Her whole body stiffened and her face turned into a scowl—her brows furrowing more and her mouth slightly opened, as if in shock.

"Queer?" she repeated back to me. "Why would you tell me that?" I stared, physically frozen.

"What will people think? They won't be okay with this. And Mom—you can't tell her," she went on, a projectile vomiting of all the things I already feared. "Maybe it's a phase. People have phases . . ." She trailed off. I felt my whole body shutting down, and couldn't look at her. I turned around, eyes watering, and rushed to my room in the basement. There, I sobbed, feeling the crushing weight of rejection. Spiralled into an endless well of self-loathing, shaming myself for being queer and wishing I was "normal." Worst of all was the guilt. As if, in being queer, I was hurting my family. My self-discovery a knife in their gut. From that day, I zipped up my mouth and decided to keep this part of me away from them. Yara and I didn't speak of it again for years, and for the time being, I abandoned my plan to tell Mom.

I knew who Tegan and Sara were in concept, having vaguely heard them in remixes on the radio. But it was Ren who taught me that they were queer icons. When they asked if I knew them, I told a half-truth, pretending I loved them. Mostly, I was tired of being a newbie to all things queer. In secret, I went to HMV and bought a bunch of their CDs. I listened to them on repeat until I knew all the words to their most popular songs. I was learning that queerness had a culture to it, much like ethnicities, religions and countries. It had its own rituals and traditions, histories and even language. For example, knowing the entire musical opening of *The L Word* was the equivalent of memorizing a national anthem. And it seemed like everyone knew that if you talked about Shane from that show, you had to mention how she did Carmen dirty. And finally, that going to a Tegan and Sara concert was a rite of passage.

For Valentine's Day, Ren wrote me a poem that I kept on my dresser, and I bought Ren tickets to see Tegan and Sara at the University of Guelph. It was one part selfish—I wanted to go, too, having learned all the lyrics. Travelling about thirty minutes, we got there hours ahead, eager to be at the front of the line. To my surprise, a few other keeners had already arrived. As time passed, I looked down the growing line, witnessing all the versions of queer you could be: the plaid button-up, outdoorsy queers; high-femme queers, with their bright lipstick and long hair; low-femme queers in their sweaters and jeans; giant-glasses-and-toque hipster queers; buzzed-undercut-and-denim-jacket queers; punk queers, with their piercings and tattoo sleeves. When the doors opened, we raced to the front of the stage, snagging a coveted spot in the centre as the room filled. As the pair walked onstage, I screamed with my whole soul.

In between sets, they told stories about their lives. They bickered. They laughed. They disagreed comically on the origin stories of songs. They talked about their early days, and what it had been like to be young queers in the music world, figuring out their identity. Watching them be so fully themselves and be celebrated in that fullness moved me to tears. The joyful kind, with a hint of yearning.

Something was shifting in me that night. I reached for Ren's hand and gazed into their eyes, genuinely excited to be near them. The only instinct in me was to get closer, to kiss their face and tell them I loved them. Then I looked at the sweaty crowd, noticing my attraction to many of them. It was like my whole life, I'd only eaten the dried fruit in a bag of trail mix. And suddenly, I felt an undeniable appetite for the almonds, and the peanuts, and the chocolate. An appetite that made me question whether I'd even liked the dried fruit all that much.

Club Renaissance was a dark and grimy queer bar that young queers and older gays would frequent equally. One night, a group of us from the Centre went. Excitedly, we pushed our bodies through the crowd until we nabbed a table in front of the stage. To our left was a solo lesbian, seemingly in her fifties—short salt-and-pepper hair gelled in a nineties style, loose leather jacket. She pointed her fingers at each of us like a finger gun, one by one: "Gay"; next person, "Gay"; and then me, "You're pretty, but not gay." "Rude," I quietly muttered under my breath, without correcting her.

The club was more Ren's thing than mine. They had capital there. Bartenders knew them by name, drag queens swam through the crowd to hug them. An hour in, Ren disappeared and emerged onstage for a drag performance. Walked onto the stage with their perfectly glued stubble, a red bandana tucked beneath their hat, and smooth boy-band moves to Childish Gambino's "Heartbeat." As Ren worked the crowd, making eye contact with others and dancing seductively, people walked up to them with bills in their mouth. Ren kneeled down, grabbing the bills with their mouth to a crowd that oohed and aahed loudly. Amidst a shrieking crowd of queers who swooned over Ren, I'll admit, I felt jealous and insecure, but also proud to be their partner.

When the drag show was done, people poured into the centre of the club. Queer folks, drag queens and drag kings, bridal parties and curious middle-aged married folk—all dancing against each other in a sweaty room. T-shirts were pulled off and lost for good. Friends and strangers disappeared into the bathroom for a cocaine break, or sex in the stalls. Some would pass out, or get caught in drunken fights, or be carried out, only to continue drinking in the parking lot, where people had left their alcohol stash behind tires and by dumpsters.

I didn't feel like I belonged at Club Renaissance, but there was something special about being there. I felt deliciously free. Like in a corner so dark, in the wee hours of the night, I could hold Ren's hand without all that gut-grumbling pain. I could kiss their face, and tell them I loved them so fucking much. I could hold their body against mine, embracing the feeling of our sweaty bodies pressed against each other. I could feel their breath against my neck, their tongue tracing the inside of my upper lip. I could hold their face and stare at them for no reason other than to stare, intently, into their green eyes as if looking at a lake. I could forget that there was anything different about us, or me. That a space like this existed, where I could do that, was profoundly radical. It was the "elsewhere" I had been looking for—not in a fantastical dimension, but here, in my real world.

12

KHARAB

I didn't think I was the kind of woman who ends a relationship over email from an ocean away, saying, *It's not you, it's me.* And if someone I loved told me that story, that some cowardly queer didn't have the guts to end it with them face to face, that they got some half-assed letter instead, saying, "I love you, but the timing isn't right," I would have called them every name in the book. It turns out I am that woman. At least, I was that woman in my early twenties.

After graduating, just a few days before leaving Waterloo, I moved all my furniture into Ren's new house. Ren had more use for it than I did, as I'd decided to live at Yara's for the next year until I figured out my next move. Ren's place was an old house with Victorian detailing, big windows, scuffed-up walls and dark wooden frames around the doors. They were elated to be moving out of their tiny one-bedroom basement into a two-floor house with a close friend. I crashed at Ren's for a week, where we argued more than we ever had. About to live in separate cities, neither of us knew whether we could make it work.

When the week was over, my mother drove in from Toronto to pick me up and celebrate my graduation. After packing my bags up and moving them to the door, Ren and I said our goodbyes inside, where my mother wouldn't see us. It was emotional for both of us, feeling the anxiousness of stepping into a new chapter of life, not knowing what was to come. Wiping away the tears, I crawled into the car with my mother, who started badgering me with questions about why I'd been staying at Ren's house instead of my own, and why I hadn't just come home when my lease was up.

Exhausted by the pressure to keep up the illusion, I eventually blurted out that Ren was my partner and I was queer. "Queer?" she asked, her face scrunching up with confusion. "Gay," I responded. "I'm gay." She paused, looking reflective as she stared straight ahead.

Overwhelmed by all the leaving—leaving Ren, leaving Waterloo, leaving school—I tried to deepen my breath, sensing a panic attack coming. I was flooded with the memory of telling Yara. The shock of her anger, how quickly she jumped to how upset others would be, especially Mom.

Eventually, Mom did respond. "Well, I love you no matter what," she said softly. When we returned home, she could barely look at me, seemingly squirming in the discomfort of what I had just shared. My confusion overshadowed the relief of finally telling the truth. Was she *really* okay with all of this? I wondered. I knew there was love in her response. I knew that so few people I knew had their parents say, in response to their coming out, that they loved them unconditionally. Yet the silence about it nagged at me. No questions about my partner, no curiosities. Neither of us mentioned it again for years. It was like the conversation had never happened.

Ren came to see me in Toronto a few weeks later, before I left to visit Iran with Mom. By then, I had grown comfortable with Ren, choosing to hold their hand because I genuinely wanted to. It felt like an anchoring—like if we just held tight enough, we could keep each other from floating away. Maybe we both felt ourselves drifting, or maybe we just sensed the clinging desperation of the other—whatever it was, we were both hanging on.

The city's inescapable summer humidity saturated the space between us, clothes sticking to skin as we wandered along uneven pavements and bustling streets. In our monotonous conversations about the city gentrifying or the way men took up too much space on the sidewalk, there was something—a simmering uncertainty—we weren't naming aloud.

My "something" was Mia. Who the hell is Mia? I had the same question. Mind you, I could find the answers; I didn't need Ren for that. This was a time when people were mindlessly posting on Tumblr and Twitter. When you could track your partner's infidelities in their comments, their hidden misogynistic or racist views by their new follows. Relationships would crash and burn over unexplained heart emojis and tagged photos. And though I gleefully critiqued our modern-day Foucauldian panopticons—cops, social workers and traffic cameras—I found great comfort in using social media as a surveillance system.

From what I could dig up, Mia was a white queer student at our school with an Australian accent. According to Twitter, when I was out of town, they would hang out. Ren said it was just the way their schedules aligned, or that I didn't need to be there all the time, or that I would meet her eventually. Half-truths you would say to someone you love, hoping they'll believe your half-truths more than you do. I started to see myself as a jealous, overbearing girlfriend with claws for hands.

Neither of us chose to name our hesitations aloud that day. Instead, we returned to the car, hands intertwined, dreaming about our future. I reassured them that we'd be walking the streets of Toronto again when I returned in two months, and I'd visit them in Waterloo. That I'd call them from Iran, and I'd write them old-fashioned romantic letters, except more like in *You've Got Mail*. And one day, we'd build a home, and it'd feel like a home. Not one of those cookie-cutter subdivision homes, but one that we'd make intentionally, with coloured cabinets and a real wooden dining table, and we'd invite our friends over for game nights.

It was one of those times that made you wonder what the difference was between a dream and a prayer. I knew that no matter what I said, something was coming undone.

I hadn't been home to Iran in more than a decade, though it was often on my mind. I would suddenly smell it in the air. I would crave my aunties' hugs, or the sound of my grandmother's laughter. Maybe it's a second-generation thing: the gut-aching grief, the melancholic fury of living in a diaspora. Sometimes, it would emerge in small moments. When the wind would momentarily graze my face with the scent of gasoline and remind me of the streets. That first bite of pomegranate seeds, that punchy tart taste on my tongue, brief before mellowing into sweetness. You learn, eventually, to honour its brevity. To accept that these reminders that transport you home will just as quickly fade, returning you to your present. I was clamouring to return to Iran that year. My heart had nudged me home with all its aching, and all these reminders.

In Farsi, when we want to say "I miss you," we say, "*Delam tangeh barat.*" Meaning "My heart is tight for you." And it was true—missing home sometimes felt hug-tight, and sometimes snake-tight—a slithering something wrapping itself around your heart, slowing it down.

This was my first trip to Tehran, where my mother had just started living. These days, Mom was secretive about her whereabouts and the general events of her life. She had barely mentioned remarrying and moving back to Iran to any of us.

In fact, one random day in the winter, when I visited her apartment in Toronto, she showed me pictures of an older man on her phone and said, "I'm married now." To this day, I have no idea how she met someone and why she decided to get married again.

Mom's new husband, Ehsan, owned a quaint apartment in a bougie neighbourhood in Tehran, overlooking the mountainous city. He wore his pants high up on the waist, and a clean, ironed dress shirt every day. Since moving back to Iran, Mom had started praying. I'd only seen her pray a handful of times in Toronto. Before we had lunch, I watched her sneak away to a room in the back and spread her prayer mat. Her hijab framed her face tightly, her freshly highlighted hair brushed back under the fabric.

Her face looked different, too. She'd always had a mole just underneath her left eye—exactly where I have a beauty mark on my face. Except now there was nothing there. When I asked her about it, she explained that Ehsan had preferred she have it removed before the marriage, and so she did. I thought it was audacious and rude to ask someone to remove something on their face, implying that it's ugly, but my mother seemed unbothered by it.

I didn't know if she was happy here, but I understood the remarriage. My mother had dreamed of a stable home, and here she was in a home with olive trees and berry bushes. Walking onto the balcony, Mom pointed out the shared pool, where a young man, likely a few years older than me, was swimming. She nudged me and said, "He's very handsome, no?" I nodded uncomfortably. "He's available, too. They're looking for a woman for him. That could be you." She smiled, continuing to nudge my arm. I moved away, irritated by the comment and trying to understand whether my mother had completely forgotten that I was queer and in a relationship with Ren, or whether she was testing whether there was still hope that I would marry a man.

This visit was just a few years after the Green Wave of Iran in 2009–10, and the call for progress was still reverberating. Protesters had taken to the streets in the largest protest since the 1979 Revolution, demanding the removal of President Mahmoud Ahmadinejad. Ahmadinejad was widely known as a highly conservative president, fond of the use of violence to control and suppress human rights. Arguably one of his most viral moments was his public statement that homosexuality didn't exist in Iran. Yes, an entire nation that simply didn't birth gays. Up until this point, there were already rumbling clashes in Iran between conservative, theocratic views and those demanding democracy and human rights. And though the protest ended in bloodshed, with mass arrests and no change to government, you couldn't deny that things were changing societally.

In Tehran, men were wearing short-sleeved t-shirts and ankle-cut pants now. Women were wearing loose hijabs with pieces of hair pulled out and colourful clothing, and some were even without a chador (cloak) or a manteau (long coat) altogether, preferring the ease of tunics. "You're allowed now?" I asked Mom, reassuring her that I wasn't about to loosen my hijab on the basis of her response. "This Iran isn't the same Iran anymore," she responded. She hadn't held a strict code of modest clothing in our home when we were growing up, nor did she keep her hijab when she moved to Canada. But even so, this cultural shift seemed unsettling to her. I could see that she, too, felt stuck between the old and new.

After a week in Tehran, we travelled to Esfahan, where I walked through the airport with a black headscarf completely covering my hair, a loose-fitting manteau and a bare face. "Do I look okay?" I asked my mother for the hundredth time, needing assurances that I was meeting the city's standards of modesty. Mom had warned me that Esfahan was different than Tehran in that it was more conservative and rigid. As we rushed from the gate to meet my family, I spotted a woman dressed entirely in black with a long chador approaching me, gesturing aggressively to stop. She stood amongst other women, dressed similarly in long black chadors and hijabs, their blazing eyes looking me up and down. "What is this? This is what you call a manteau? This is far too short to be worn in public," she said, brows furrowed.

Before she could continue, a chorus of voices from my aunties to my cousins chimed in to explain that I was "*khareji*," meaning an outsider or foreigner. That I should be forgiven for not yet knowing the rules of modesty here. This was, of course, the bullshit women regularly fed the *Gasht-e-Ershad*, also known as the women's morality police. My cousins were no strangers to these people, who regularly policed women and girls who transgressed their conservative ideas around Muslim womanhood. Their vigilance reminded me of the very real threat of imprisonment and even death that loomed above women, especially those who dared to defy their rules. Following their lead, I said, "I don't know what you're telling me. I'm from CA-NA-DA."

When they finally released me on a warning, I was swept into the arms of my cousins and aunties. "*SAAAA-LAAAAAAAMMMMM*," Khaleh Soraya said the way she always did, stretching her words like sweet dough, savouring each syllable. She pressed her hands against my cheeks, staring into my eyes before pulling me into her body, hands wrapped tightly around my shoulders. New wrinkles and freckles had appeared on her skin since the last time I'd seen her, and old ones had deepened. Her oversized round glasses were a whimsical new addition; she pointed to them and said,

"I'm getting old now." I held on to her tightly, feeling over-joyed to return to her. In that moment, we didn't speak in words; no, we spoke in bodies. In tears that soaked through her manteau, leaving grief stains. In the tightness of our hands, refusing to let go. In the slowing of our breath, in the quivering of our lips, in the way gravity hugged our feet.

On the drive home, I took a whiff of the air and closed my eyes, exactly as I had done over a decade ago. This time, wanting to savour it all. It was exactly as I remembered it—the smell of gasoline, of humidity and freshly cut greenery. I breathed in deeply, taking it all in and feeling immediately peaceful.

Very little had changed amongst my family since my last visit. I spent most of my days at Khaleh Soraya's house, while my mother stayed with my grandmother instead. Though all my aunties were warm and affectionate, I felt most connected to Khaleh Soraya. In the mornings, I would join her in the kitchen, where she was pulling things out of the fridge for our breakfast. One by one, I carried them to the spread, laying out the *noon barbari*, feta cheese, parsley, butter and jam. Together, we sat in a peaceful quiet, drinking our *chai shireen* (sweet tea) and layering our bread with different variations of the ingredients. In the afternoons, my cousin Amin would come home for a mid-afternoon siesta. But first, we would play a few rounds of cards, like old times. And for dinner, we would drive over to my grandmother's, where everyone in the family would crowd, pouring out into the front yard, too. The joyful sound of kids playing, of music booming and soulful laughter. On many days, my Amou Javid would stop by for some tea and a round of cards, too. "What is this, kid? Is the plan to only visit us every ten years?" he chuckled with the same staccato laughter as before. I hugged him tightly, as if I was trying to make up for lost time.

The fact that I was now a grown adult meant that I was seeing Iran through a different lens, too. During our visits to bazaars and historic sites, I became acutely aware of the large-scale images of Ayatollah Khomeini that scattered the streets. His intensely stern eyes were everywhere. "Why is he everywhere now?" I asked my mother one day during a visit to a local bazaar, and she responded that surely I had seen these before, as they'd been here for decades. Clearly, my enamoured feelings towards Iran the last time had clouded my view, leaving me with an idealistic portrait of it. "I feel like he's always watching me," I commented, disturbed by his gaze. Continuing our walk, I noticed the morality police walking the streets and made my body smaller, collapsing into Khaleh Soraya as if to hide behind her chador. Even though I was dressed perfectly "proper" by their standards, I still felt this pervasive anxiety of being caught for something.

It reminded me of Foucault's writings on Jeremy Bentham's panopticon, an architectural structure of a prison whereby there's a central tower with a guard who surveils the inmates. He writes, "the major effect of the Panopticon [is] to induce in the inmate a state of conscious and permanent visibility that assures the automatic functioning of power."[2] In other words, constant surveillance, whether it be real or perceived, results in regulation, in people falling into line. It functions effectively because we internalize that gaze, and we discipline ourselves accordingly. It was ironic that Ayatollah Khomeini and his regime would mirror this approach to perpetuate the feeling of constant surveillance. Particularly because Foucault, a critic of the panoptican, had written fondly of Ayatollah Khomeini in the seventies, even

2. Michel Foucault, *Discipline and Punish: The Birth of the Prison*, trans. Alan Sheridan [1977] (New York: Vintage, 1995), 201.

visiting him at his home in France. His articles critiqued the Shah's authoritarian policies and romanticized Ayatollah Khomeini's political Islamism, dismissing the voices of feminists who sounded alarms around Khomeini.

Distressing to me was the way in which the anti-woman sentiments of the regime had trickled into my family. The older generation would talk about *zaneh kharab* this and *zaneh kharab* that. *Kharab* was a word you would traditionally use for food, to mean rotten, or objects, to mean broken. The apple is kharab. The car is kharab. Last night's dinner is kharab. I had never heard of people being kharab. *Zaneh kharab* directly translated to "women who are rotten or broken."

According to my relatives, *zaneh kharab* was a category of women that you didn't want to be lumped in with. They were the kind of women who threatened to steal your husband at a bazaar and leave you raising your three children alone, broke and sad. They were the kind of women who wore loose hijabs that almost rested at their neck. The kind of women who wore barely-there manteaus, who drank alcohol, or worse, smoked crystal meth. The kind of women who had boyfriends, who had sex out of wedlock and lied their way into marriages with innocent men who had no idea of their dark histories. They were sex workers, and addicts, and, really, any woman who refused to abide by Islamic law in ways the older generation of my family saw fit. And though they didn't say it, queer women were most certainly kharab.

While my cousins were more progressive, it wasn't uncommon for my aunties to point out women and call them *zaneh kharab* amongst themselves on our car rides. The anxiety I felt on the streets now crept into my interactions with my family, too. I wondered if they could see it in me—that I, too, was by their standards a rotten woman. I tried not to ask too many questions, fearing that questions would lead to suspicion about me.

Mid-afternoon on a weekday, laughter filled the air at my Khaleh Bahar's house. I was drinking chai as my mother and aunties shared stories about their younger years. "You know, Khaleh Bahar was a hippie. She would wear a chador on the way out of the house, then take it off outside, a miniskirt underneath." Mom laughed, pointing at her eldest sister. "What about you?" I asked her. "I wouldn't dare—I always dressed proper, with a *maghnaeh* for school," she responded, referring to a tighter, more conservative hijab that schoolgirls now wore. "But I liked it—I wanted to dress like that, too," she said.

"Do you remember that day?" Khaleh Soraya asked Mom, referencing a day when Mom was maybe ten or twelve years old, waiting for Dayee Shahin to return home. She stuck her bare head outside the window to watch for him. Often, she was excited for him to come home, knowing that he would liven up the space. Dayee Shahin, walking down the street, saw her hair blowing in the wind and rushed into the house with rage. "He was very angry. He hit me so much, yelling, 'Why are you without hijab? People can see you outside!'"

"He hit you?" I asked, horrified by the story. "Where were your parents?"

"Baba Ali and Khanoom lived a good life back then." She chuckled with her sisters. "Always travelling or with friends. It was always Shahin taking care of us. And he would—he really took care of us," she emphasized.

The sisters changed the subject, instead recalling the sweet moments between them. Like how Shahin would slide into the living room, where the sisters were talking, smile conspiratorially and say, "So, who are we gossiping about today?" Or how the family would gather in the home and he would read

Hafiz or Khayyam. That's how they all preferred to remember him—in his joy, laughing and making others laugh.

I'd begun to understand how terribly complicated it had been for Mom to be, essentially, raised by her brother. That she'd felt both protected and cared for by Shahin, and also deeply impacted by his rage, his aggression, his violence. But it was only later, during the Jin, Jian, Azadi (Woman, Life, Freedom) movement in Iran, which began in 2022 following the death of an Iranian Kurdish woman, Zhina/Mahsa Amini, in police custody, that I started asking Mom more questions about her family's ideas about women's liberation. Amini had been arbitrarily arrested by the morality police for wearing an "improper" hijab. After being violently assaulted by police, she fell into a coma and tragically died later at the hospital. People courageously flooded the streets of Iran, risking their lives to demand an end to the regime. Diasporic Iranians and allies rose up, too, in protest against the Islamic Republic and its ongoing gender apartheid, where women are continuously denied full rights of participation in society.

"What about women's freedom? Did he believe in that?" I asked my mother, curious, about where women fit into Dayee Shahin's idea of a Muslim democracy. According to her, Dayee Shahin believed that a Muslim democracy would lead them to class equity, which, to him, was freedom. "Women were free, too," she shrugged. I probed further. "But wasn't he very specific about what women could and couldn't do?" She agreed that he was, and laid out a list of examples, prefaced with his belief that his sisters had to reflect the Muslim values he held, in the way he believed they should be practised. For example, shoes with soft, soundless soles were mandatory. No thin leggings, no makeup. A hijab was to be worn at all times outside or, even better, a chador. Laughing with men outside was *haram* (forbidden), as was walking on the same side of the street as men when going to school. No visits to stores alone, and no men staring at you. There was to be no going to people's homes, or sleepovers. And if non-familial men were in the home, the women were to go to a different room. "And what would happen if you didn't follow those rules?" I asked. "Oh, he would be so angry. Sometimes hitting. Sometimes yelling," she responded, again nonchalantly.

I recalled my mother telling me that she hadn't experienced violence before my father, that it wasn't the norm in her family. But the truth was changing now; she hadn't seen it with her parents, but she certainly had with her eldest brother.

I hesitated to say what I was thinking—that Dayee Shahin had been controlling, and dominating, and abusive. Instead, I said, "I'm sure you loved him, and that he was caring in a lot of ways. But he sounds angry and violent."

"Yeah, but I would push him. I was always making him think, *What about women?* or disagreeing with him," she responded, trying to explain it away quickly.

"So, did you want to wear a hijab, or did he make you?" I asked her, trying to sift through where my mother's agency ended and where his control had begun.

"I wanted to wear a hijab because it was a choice, then. Not a lot of people were wearing it. But when it became mandatory, I didn't want it anymore. I wanted to choose," she explained.

It was clear that her brother had demanded a particular performance of womanhood that, in some ways, aligned with Mom's perspectives, and in others, drastically didn't. And though Mom felt she had full bodily autonomy, I wondered how much of her behaviour as a child and teenager, wearing a tight maghnaeh to school and dressing conservatively, was about the safety she was granted when complying with Shahin.

Over that 2013 summer in Iran, Khaleh Soraya became my *qibla*, my moral compass. "What kind of hijab is that?" I asked her, gesturing towards a group of young girls dressed in all black. Sure, I was curious, but I also knew my question would impress her.

"Those are schoolkids. They wear the maghnaeh," she responded.

"I like their hijab." I smiled and realized I had forgotten what a maghnaeh looked like. Khaleh gazed at me with an approving smile. Days later, I found myself a black maghnaeh at the bazaar. I started dressing for God, with long-sleeved shirts and a knee-length manteau in the high heat of the summer. I even donned a chador a few times, just like Khaleh Soraya would wear. My aunties looked at my mother like *Damn, you raised this dream of a child?*

I kept thinking, *This place could be your forever home, if you could just make yourself fit.* I even started thinking that I could marry a man here and leave behind my complicated queer life. The truth was, the juiciness of home and belonging had me imagining all sorts of shit I hadn't thought I'd wanted. Shit I'd thought I was too progressive for, too radical for.

Not everyone was as devoutly and conservatively Muslim as Khaleh Soraya. Many of my cousins weren't. There was my cousin Manijeh, who was part of the younger generation of Muslim women that devoutly believed in both Allah and women's rights. She painted her eyelids with the boldest of eyeshadows and wore loose, colourful hijabs with her high-lighted curls peeking through the front.

Manijeh lived on the second floor of a quaint apartment that I loved visiting on quiet midweek days. On a Wednesday afternoon, we sat at a small wooden dining table in her white-tiled kitchen, laughing as she picked apart the Los Angeles Persian music videos, with their luxury cars and scantily dressed women. That was, until I started to sob into my perfectly cooked *gheimeh*. "What happened? Do you miss

home? You must miss home," Manijeh asked, naturally concerned. With a mouth full of half-chewed lentils and rice, and
mascara streaking my cheeks, I hunched over and cried an
even bigger cry.

It wasn't that I missed home; it was that I really didn't
want to go home. I was suddenly *seriously* considering marrying
a man and moving to Iran, where I could be surrounded by my
beloved family. Nothing in Canada could remotely compare to
the feeling of folding into the soft bodies of my aunties, who
would press their faces against mine and tell me they loved me.
Or the generosity of my cousins, who would cook me gheimeh.
Who would hold my hand as we walked the streets, always
poking fun at each other and laughing.

When my breath returned, I asked Manijeh how she knew
if a woman was kharab. To me, in that moment, this was the
only barrier—that I wouldn't be marriage material. "You're
not kharab! Sure, you're *khareji*, but you're not kharab! We
have different beliefs, different cultures," she reassured me.
"No, but how do you know?" I asked. Manijeh paused briefly
before explaining that some are more obvious than others—
the sex workers living on the streets, those with addictions.
"But what if a woman used to be kharab, but now she's good?
How would you know?" I wondered aloud. Manijeh explained
that sometimes you would hear about their histories from
others in the neighbourhood, or families would have doctors
check the hymen and it would be broken. I became obsessed
with finding a loophole.

"What if a woman has used tampons?"

"What if a woman rode a horse and her hymen broke?"

"What if a woman was just born with a broken hymen?"

Whether it was intentional or by chance, a broken hymen
was enough to fold you into the *zaneh kharab* category. As was
my being queer, which, regardless of how much I tried to conceal

it, I thought they would just know. The reality was that the confines of what made a good woman were always this suffocating and sharp. Yet I wanted to belong. I edged myself closer and closer to the edges of the box, willing to cut off whole parts of me, willing to make myself smaller if it meant I could belong with them and stay here, in the land of good women.

That same week, I wrote Ren an email with the same tired explanations I'd heard in the movies. Stuff about growing apart and no longer wanting to be with them, and some abstruse allusion to there being more to the story. The pressure to be acceptable had intensified to a boiling point. In my mind, to stay here, I had to be a good Iranian woman. And to be a good Iranian woman, I had to be a good Muslim. And that would require me to sacrifice my queerness.

In my efforts to distance myself from my queerness, I told myself I was only queer by association—that it had been a rite of passage, a youthful and naive exploration of sexuality that all of us went through. I exiled the things I thought "made" me queer—plaid shirts, political pins, books. My partner, my friends, even the city I deemed the birthplace of my "gay." I swore off drag clubs. I promised to get right with God. And I told myself, again and again: *I was never really gay, anyway.*

13

SHAME

At twenty-two, I flung myself as far away from my family as I could, moving across the country to Vancouver to do a master's degree in English literature. For the past year, I had lived a rather mundane life at Yara's home in Toronto—single, working, saving money for graduate school. Queerness was something I had left in the past since returning from Iran. Yasaman was living a couple hours north of the city and now had two kids, and I rarely saw or spoke to my dad. And Mom was going back and forth between Toronto and Tehran with her husband. I looked to the West Coast city as my spiritual mecca, delivering me to my pre-existing goodness—you know, before my damning queer year.

When my old friend Daphne, who I'd met in a feminist circle in Waterloo, ended up in Vancouver for grad school, too, I was determined to redefine myself to her as straight. Daphne was an endearing and gloriously nerdy white woman with a passion for the arts. I knew her as half of a pair: where Daphne was, Cee was. Cee was a quirky white woman who stood out in any crowd. Bright-blond hair, pale skin and deep Christian roots. They had one of those rare Millennial stories where they met in an online chat room, developed a meaningful relationship and actually were who they said they were. It was unheard of. They'd been fully themselves, and lucky enough to become each other's halves.

The two attended the same program at Laurier, and after a year or so of spending every waking moment together, they realized they were in love. There really is a God, I remembered thinking.

When I first saw Daphne in Vancouver, I hoped she wouldn't ask me about Ren. Sure enough, she did, but I was prepared. "Oh, I'm not queer anymore," I said. Before she could settle into confusion and questions, I asked: "And Cee?" I sensed an untethering between them. Had they been together, I imagined she would have been here, too.

She explained that Cee had broken up with her and moved out to a small religious community, where she was no longer identifying as queer. "Damn," I responded, my mouth gaping open. It made me angry that Cee would up and leave Daphne like that. Kind, sweet Daphne. The irony of my anger was lost on me; I was unable to see that Cee and I weren't so different. Both trying to pray away the gay, to obsessively scrub ourselves clean of our *haram* pasts. I think Daphne knew it, even if I couldn't see it. Or wouldn't. As for my own queerness, I gave Daphne a spontaneously crafted story about being into men now.

I met Clementine at a pub after our program orientation, where a group of us English graduate students gathered for drinks. At first glance, she was your typical West Coaster. A thin white woman with long brown hair who could potentially be a ballet dancer, or perhaps a Pilates instructor. I can't remember what we were talking about, but I remember her saying, "I get Botox." And a few breaths later, "for my migraines, of course." She paused and smirked, and we both laughed.

Clementine felt one part intellectual, one part theatre, one part reality show. I took comfort in how weird she was. She had an obsession with cacti because she had dreamed once that her deceased father had been reincarnated as a cactus. Much of what she owned was covered in imagery of cacti. Of course, that was before the onset of her obsession with Benedict Cumberbatch, after which much of what she owned was plastered with his face. Her Halloween costume that year was Benedict Lumberbatch—her plaid take on Benedict. When Clementine loved something, she truly loved it. It was what I loved most about her. She went hard for love.

A few weeks into my time in Vancouver, I went out to a local pub for drinks with friends, including Clementine. I met a guy, gave him my number and, later on, drunkenly invited him back to my place. When he arrived at my door, I began to regret the decision. But instead of leaving him outside, I let him in. And after a terribly painful sexual encounter with him, I let him fall asleep in my bed, thankful that it was over with. The next morning, when I tried to get him to leave, he pushed for more sex and I said no, desperate not to go through it all again. But he wouldn't accept my no. "I have needs," he proclaimed, pulling my frozen body towards him and starting again.

That morning, I sat at my dining table in a tear-stained oversized sweater, preparing to call Clementine, and wondering how to explain that I'd been sexually assaulted by the guy I'd met the night before. A thing I wanted to forget. But on the call, Clementine didn't question me; all that mattered was what I needed now. You never really know how much someone cares for you until they hop in their car, drive to a drugstore and get you the morning-after pill at nine a.m. on a Sunday.

Clementine walked into my apartment, dropped her bag to the ground and immediately pulled me in. I don't know how long we stood like that, her holding me in her arms tightly as I cried.

We sat quietly in her bright-red Mini Cooper as she zipped across the city to the hospital, where we knew there was a sexual violence unit. At that point she barely knew me, but she was there for me—in the waiting room, in the examination room, to do my HIV test, to return home that day. It was the kind of care that would define platonic love for me. Where all you can do is be there, and so that's what you do.

I wanted to call Yara that day, but the last time we'd spoken about anything vulnerable was when I came out to her. I didn't think she would know how to be there for me. Not in the way that I needed her to be. Not in a way that was gentle, and patient, and kind. And even though she wasn't there, and she didn't know, I could hear her as clearly as I heard her that day. *How could you let this happen? Why would you tell me this?* My woundings, my vulnerabilities always seemed to irritate her, bringing out a harsher, less compassionate side of her. The kindest thing I could do for her and myself was to never tell her. My silence, a gift.

Even though Clementine reassured me that there was nothing I'd done wrong, I played back the scenario over and over again. Had I not been drinking, maybe this wouldn't have happened. Had I not talked to him at the bar, maybe this wouldn't have happened. Had I not given him my number. Had I not looked his way. Had I not smiled. Had I not invited him in. Had I not been wearing a skirt. Had I not, had I not, had I not.

I had grown up with the clear idea that good things happened to good girls. Or at least, that's what I was told. That good girls don't get drugged. Good girls don't get raped. Good girls don't end up in hospitals, with rape kits and social workers and nurses asking, "Do you want to keep a sample, so that if you ever want to press charges, you have something?" Good girls don't need Plan B. Good girls are protected by God.

Trauma had sunk me into the land of the dead, where I barely existed. Dissociation swallowed me whole, so much that I rarely knew what was happening in class. I was once told that dissociation is an act of love. That the body loves you so immensely, it refuses to have you be present for the pain of living. It taps you out, entirely. It takes you somewhere else— somewhere untouchable. Dissociation was, in many ways, a familiar friend.

In class, I began to fall apart and failed to meet the gruelling expectations of the program. The curiosity and joy with which I'd once approached cultural critics and psychoanalytic theories were hollowing out. Instead, where there was once joy, there was numbness—and when numbness would relent, there was unfiltered pain. I would sit towards the back of the class, head down, tuned out. Mid-class, I would spontaneously start shaking. Unable to focus, I would try to excuse myself. Some days, I left with ease—parking myself in the bathroom, where I would weep quietly in a stall until I felt numb again.

The one thing I was good at—school—was disappearing. I knew how to be polite. I knew how to finish my work. I knew how to read. I knew how to participate, fully and enthusiastically. I knew how to do all of this, and yet I couldn't. Not anymore.

A few months after I was sexually assaulted, I swiped right on the man who had assaulted me. His profile as generic as any twenty-something white dude's. A picture with his crew of white bros, who probably called him "broski," a picture with a pint of beer and a picture out in nature, not a fish photo but something that said "I'm a man" no less. I felt my left hand bunch into a fist. Inside me, the rumblings of two parts sparring. The bitter demands of one yelling, "Swipe left and move on!" The quiet whisper of another wondering if he would even remember me.

With a gentle flick of my finger, I invited him back into my life. When he asked me out for dinner, I blushed like a teenager and said yes. I was excited, even. I convinced myself that maybe I'd been wrong about that night, or he hadn't heard me say no, or I wasn't remembering it right, or it wasn't that bad. That I was overreacting, and that sometimes people do that. The next evening, I spent two hours getting ready for our date. Perfectly pinning in my hair extensions, blending my eyeshadow, wearing something that read sexy but sweet. I couldn't tell anyone about it. My mouth couldn't form the words. Not even to Clementine.

I took a forty-minute bus ride to his neighbourhood, and by the time I got there, the sky had started spitting. Of course I had forgotten my seventh umbrella on a bus. I waited at the corner for twenty minutes, taking shelter at the bus stop and returning to the corner again and again.

When he finally arrived, he chuckled that he lived a mere ten minutes away and found it funny that I still got there before him. I remember saying, "Oh, it's okay. It happens," even though he wasn't apologizing or asking for my compassion. My hair soaked, I chuckled along with him. I looked at his face, trying to remember what I'd seen in him that night.

"So . . . where're we going?"

"Uh—over here."

He gestured to a takeout burger joint ten steps away, with a line already forming outside it. We stood there, barely speaking to each other, and he stared at my face. I told myself it was because I looked pretty that night.

Fifteen minutes into waiting, he smiled, opened his mouth and said: "You know—I'm not sure you're gonna be worth it." "What do you mean?" I coyly responded. "I mean, I don't know if I'm gonna pay tonight. I don't know if you're worth it," he said. I walked away. I looked back once, to see him walking in the opposite direction. There would be no redemption story here, no powerful moment of reclaiming agency.

Years later, I would tell my friends this story, except I would always change the details. Never from the beginning. Chopped up, mixed and blended. Unrecognizable against the real story. I would tell it and retell it until I convinced myself it was a comical date-night anecdote and nothing else. The story of a naive twenty-something girl, or the story of some asshole out there in the world. Sometimes, I'd tell it as if it was some hipster dude I'd thought had a soft side because he swore he was a feminist and would fuck up anyone who stepped to his sister. Or I'd change it to the story of me dating a white lesbian who declared themself "colour-blind" and claimed their ex was "a psycho." Those *are* real people I've dated, just not the ones in this story.

No matter how much I cut that story up, how much I tried to rewrite it or disappear it altogether, it haunted me. It made me believe I was just a woman with a big imagination, making it all up. Nobody has dinner with their rapist, Roza. No one returns to the site of wreckage that painful. No one does.

The feminist scholar Sara Ahmed writes that shame requires a witness. That the imagined view of someone witnessing our perceived badness is enough. Maybe, by altering and obscuring the details of that encounter, I thought I was outsmarting shame. If shame needed a witness, I would deny it that. I would chop up the truth so finely, it would become unrecognizable to others. I wonder: Had Mom been doing the same with all those stories about her brother, a heroic man who could do no wrong?

For years I tried to make it make sense. If I could, then maybe I could tell the story straight. Maybe some part of me wanted to reach into the past and rip the page out. Or maybe I wanted to write the story anew. Like, this isn't a tale of trauma; it's one of repair. Or maybe, it's a story about how trauma makes us do wild things.

No matter how I've told it, it's never felt redemptive or cleansing; but in time, I've accepted that the truth might never feel that way. Instead, I imagine that young woman in her early twenties, buried in shame, and I muster every ounce of compassion in my bones to remind her: It was never your fault. You were always worthy of dignity and respect.

14

UNICORN

"I'm done with men," I vented to Clementine, who hyped me up at her house, Benedict Cumberbatch memorabilia scattered everywhere. The night before, a group of us from the graduate program had gone out for drinks and stopped by a shawarma shop. Michael, a white dude from the suburbs of Calgary, had fixated on my pronunciation of shawarma. "No, it's not 'sha-warma,' it's 'shwww-arma,'" he explained. And it kept going— "I have a Turkish friend; that's how they pronounce it, too." It may have been a minor, forgettable detail in the overarching story of my life if men hadn't corrected me so often, if I hadn't just been sexually assaulted by a man, and if I wasn't already angry.

Mid-vent, it occurred to me that I didn't actually have to endure men explaining things to me. I didn't actually have to endure relationships with men, period. And so I abruptly swore off them.

I recognize that this would be difficult for many, but at the time, it felt really easy. I had few examples of loving, tender men in my life—with the exception of my Amou Javid and Baba Ali. I pulled away from the graduate student festivities. I even stopped watching my beloved romantic comedies. Instead, I watched Xavier Dolan films.

I watched *I Killed My Mother* more times than I could count. There was something intriguing about seeing such relentless rage towards a mother. I had always been soft-tongued with mine, my rage often repressed by the unbearable guilt of feeling any anger towards her. It's not that rage towards a mother was foreign to me; I grew up with Yasaman, after all, who often violated the basic cultural obligations of daughterhood. And given her failure to be a good daughter, I saw myself as doubly responsible for the happiness of my mother.

Depression had left me a lot of time to be moody and introspective about our family dynamics. The more introspective I was, the more rage towards my mother reared its head, until finally, we barely spoke. I told myself that if I had accepted my queerness, the assault never would have happened. And I blamed Mom and Yara, convinced that if they had been more supportive when I came out, I would never have swayed back to the straight path. Of course, in retrospect, my logic was flawed. For one thing, sexual violence happens in queer communities, too.

Scattered across campus were queer posters by a non-profit, taped up to poles and bulletin boards. Each with a photograph of a person or two, with text overlaid, narrating a set of facts about them. There were elder queers, and queers in love, and solo queers, and queer pals. One in particular caught my eye: an architecture student who loved eating *ghormeh sabzi*, a traditional Iranian stew, and teaching her younger cousins Farsi. The name in the corner was "Bahar." *Shit, there's a Bahar out there?* I thought. Some queer Persian living so free and comfortable she put her face on a campaign that was practically everywhere on campus? At that point, I had erased all proof of my own queerness and deleted all my old social media accounts. The Millennial equivalent of burning all your old love letters and photos. I couldn't fathom that level of visibility.

A few weeks later, I heard that Professor E, who I'd studied under at Laurier, was going to be giving a talk on diaspora and queerness at my university. He was a queer person of colour, living a life that I was aching for at the time. A tenure-track teaching position, a loving partner, a life in Toronto. When I first saw the email about his panel, I ignored it. It's hard to see anything when you're drowning in depression, let alone a life jacket being thrown at you. But when Professor E reached out himself to invite me to the event, I felt obligated to accept.

The panel was in a small lecture hall, and it included the most people of colour I had seen in one room at the university. There were other speakers, queer people of colour living in diaspora, speaking of the complexities of their experience. Em, a queer community organizer, talked at length about how organizers were burning out and the city was losing its queer spaces. When the talk was done, I hurried myself over to Em and uttered words that I hadn't allowed myself to say in over a year: "I'm Roza, and I'm queer." She handed over a card with her information on it and invited me to connect.

The next week, Em and I sat in a coffee shop at the corner of Main and Broadway, just down the street from the café she organized at. "You should come out to Femme Fridays," she said. *Femme*. I don't think I'd heard the word before. And if I had, it had never felt so delicious, so resonant. I couldn't ask what *femme* was, for fear that I'd be giving away the fact that I was a baby queer, and that was somehow a shameful thing. Whatever it was, I knew I was "it" enough to be invited into the space.

I told her how I'd struggled with finding queer community, especially as a queer of colour whose only experience was in almost entirely white spaces. I left out the part that said "I've spent the last year cosplaying a straight woman because I thought God would hate me, and felt I owed my mom straightness for her sacrifices." It felt too vulnerable for day one of a friendship.

"I've never met another queer Iranian," I told her. "I'm starting to think they don't exist—I feel like I'm a unicorn."

"Oh my god! I KNOW a unicorn! Mahshid. She's Iranian!"

"Oh. My. GOD!"

"I should connect you two! That would be so cute."

A few weeks later, I met the unicorn. Mahshid showed up at a hip Lebanese restaurant in Gastown. I walked in and yelled, "You're the unicorn!" "I'm the unicorn!" Mahshid laughed back. A few minutes in, and that's when I realized it. Goddamn, I was in the presence of a queer celebrity. "Bahar" from the posters. It would take months before either of us brought it up.

We tucked into a corner of the dimly lit restaurant like old friends. Mahshid had short dark hair, olive skin and a whimsically expressive face. She dragged her hellos out so long they wrapped around you like a blanket, just as my aunties and cousins did back home. She tracked time through haircuts and colourings, musing over whether something had happened in her blond-hair days or her red-hair days. She seemed like a genuinely good person. Not good like follow-the-rules, but good like fuck-the-rules, you are more import-ant. She hugged like my aunties, pulling me in with both arms and holding me there in a brief pause—not out of obli-gation, but out of sincere joy to see me. Her half-moon eyes meeting my half-moon eyes. It was like I had known her for years.

Like she was an old friend, I told her everything. From being queer, to not being queer, to being queer again. The academic program I now struggled to finish. The sexual assault. Everything. "Man, Vancouver has *not* been good to you," Mahshid said, disappointed in a city that she had both great love for and complicated feelings about. With her, I slowly started to unfurl.

Though Mahshid was only a few years older than me, she had elder-queer energy. Her home felt like an *adult* home, scattered with souvenirs like a street sign from Kerman, a city in Iran. I sat comfortably on her couch as she offered me everything and anything in her pantry. "What about sour keys?" she finally asked, holding up a giant Costco-sized container that reminded me of my Scarborough days. This was the start of a tradition where I would show up at her house, grab a sour key from the tub and get cozy on the couch.

She had just glowingly returned from Iran, the smell of home still on her skin. She loved going back, where her aunts and uncles and cousins would shower her with love and affection. I wondered about how she travelled back home without any qualms or worries as an openly queer person. "How do you do it?" I asked her, wanting to take notes. "I never use my real name in anything queer-related," she started, going on to name the many ways she existed under the radar. "And what about back home? Does your family know you're queer?" I hesitated asking her this, feeling that it may be too sensitive or personal. "I don't hide it," she responded, making it clear that she came from a family that loved her so fully, they didn't care that she was queer. The Revolution had turned some families more conservative than they'd ever been before, and other families, more liberal. Hers had swung left. A part of me felt salty that my family had swung right. I couldn't imagine a world where I didn't conceal my queerness.

That night, Mahshid shared stories about Iran and I listened like a child to a fairy tale. She talked about an Iran I had never known, nor known existed. One where there were underground parties and alternative spaces. Punk women with inked-up arms. Skaters with longboards drifting through the streets. Poets and artists redefining the limits of expression under a hyper-conservative Islamic regime. And one where you could find queer lesbians sprawled out at certain parks, a portrait of lovers in a field, hidden from the regime's eyes.

"You saw gays?"

"Yeah!"

"You saw gays? . . . In Iran?"

"Yeah! There are gays in Iran!"

I don't know why it had never occurred to me that there were, of course, gays in Iran. It was obvious that there were. It would be statistically impossible for there to be an entire country with no gays. Yet as naive as it may sound, I had it in my mind that we just didn't exist outside the diaspora. That I was a unicorn.

Meeting Mahshid marked the beginnings of my curiosity about queerness both in pre-modern and modern Iran, and eventually my discovery of both Afsaneh Najmabadi and Janet Afary's eye-opening research on gender and sexuality. Much like the ancient Greeks, Iranians didn't classify desire and relationships within the confines of heterosexuality and homosexuality during the medieval and early modern periods. While they viewed the Quran as prohibiting same-sex relationships, these relationships continued existing within the bounds of certain sexual conventions and mores. Not recognized and affirmed as equally valid, but rather, tolerated.

I embraced these histories, but it would be inaccurate to paint the pre-modern and early modern era of Iran as a queer utopia. For example, Afary notes that amongst men, same-sex relations had to be "asymmetrical, involving people of different ages, classes, or social standings."[3] With that said, there were also beloved stories reflected in Sufi literature where courtships were between people more equal. Most known is the story of Rumi and the mystic Mawlana Shams Tabrizi; some suspect they were lovers, though this was never proven.

Thrilling to me were the stories of brotherhood and sisterhood *sighehs*—pronounced "see-gheh," and meaning courtship practices—which were documented from the seventeenth century into the twentieth. According to Afary, "Sisterhood vows seemed to have been common between elite urban women."[4] These courtships between women were permitted amongst married folks and could be sexual and non-sexual companionships, with homosocial or homosexual overtones. As part of the courtship, whether sexual or platonic, it was customary for women to spend time together for months prior to sisterhood vows, exchanging gifts and planning brief trips.

I blushed as I read a particular passage in Afary's research naming a tradition where women could go to a love broker, seeking a woman.[5] The love broker would then go to the prospective woman with a tray of sweets, which in the middle had either a wax or leather doll or a dildo. The prospective woman would place either a black scarf atop the tray, which meant no, or a sequined white one, which meant yes. It had been hard for me to imagine same-sex desire beyond the contemporary period, let alone the development of traditions associated with it.

General ignorance about such histories isn't unsurprising, given attempts by various folks in power to conceal and minimize their existence. In uncovering them, I was also unravelling and discovering myself, newly seeing myself within a larger

3. Janet Afary, *Sexual Politics in Modern Iran* (Cambridge: Cambridge University Press, 2009), 79.
4. Afary, *Sexual Politics*, 90, 101.
5. Afary, *Sexual Politics* Ibid., 102.

context. I suddenly felt less alone as I imagined queer ancestors within my own lineage. The stunning visual of distant aunties courting other women, falling in love and, eventually, taking vows. My queerness a reclamation of an identity that had long existed. It was something I was claiming for *us*, not just myself. In witnessing Mahshid, it began to seem possible that my Iranian identity could co-exist peacefully with my sexuality. Anchoring into that truth, I started to move beyond the question of *Am I queer?* to *Who am I as a queer person?*

I found the courage to march into Femme Friday alone. I followed my natural impulse to spend hours beforehand googling what *femme* actually meant, how a femme dresses and how to talk about femme identity. I was afraid of getting it wrong. One leather jacket, pair of black jeans, black shirt and smear of red lipstick later, I arrived at Heartwood. Standing outside, I peered into the space and glowed at the sight. The room was buzzing with high femmes and soft femmes and hard femmes and non-binary femmes. There were bold lipstick and heels, tattooed arms and frilly shirts, blazers and crop pants, hipster toques and giant glasses, plaid shirts and plain jeans. Femmes with body hair and femmes with none. All kinds of bodies, all kinds of races, all kinds of faces.

I walked towards Em, who was already in conversation with a few others. A tall white woman in her forties with curly salt-and-pepper hair, a brunette with a pixie cut and glorious knee-high boots, a brown femme with long dark hair and round glasses that screamed *artist*. Em immediately invited me into the circle, introducing me to each person like I was the new kid at school. Each of them took their time inviting me into conversation, giving me the down-low and what's-what in Vancouver.

By the end of the night, I mused on how diverse the queer community felt in this city. Here, there was no "perfect" way of being. Here, femme was yours to define. Here, everyone belonged. It was youthful naïveté to see the community in such an idyllic way. Yet at the time, I clung to that story, unwilling to see anything other than a queer utopia.

A couple weeks later, I went back to that same café where Femme Fridays were held. It was a sunny day, and the Heartwood was en route home. I heard someone say, "Oh man, you just missed Tegan and Sara. They were sitting right here." The moment felt spiritual, like a sign from the universe proclaiming "You are exactly where you are supposed to be; you are exactly who you're supposed to be."

In December, I flew home to Toronto. Yara picked me up at the airport, looking excited to see me, and drove me to her house, where I'd be staying. Mom had moved into a one-bedroom apartment with Ehsan just down the street from Yara's. There was no room for me there.

For Christmas dinner, Yara and Yasaman both had plans at their in-laws', so I was the only one to go to Mom's. Her apartment was a confluence of old and new. Aging, clunky leather couches and a familiar coffee table crowded their tiny living room. A new Persian rug sprawled across the entire space, and there was a dining table for six.

Her half-moon eyes sparkled when she opened the door to me. She pulled me in quickly and rushed over to her rice on the stove. I understood why. A minute too long, and the rice would become mush. The smell of roasted chicken in the air, fresh fruit, *salad-e Shirazi*.

Ehsan hobbled over to the door with a bright smile on his face. I shook his hand and he returned himself to the couches, sitting quietly and watching the Iranian programming on the television.

"Eat something, eat something. Do you want tea? I'll make you tea," Mom said, with an unfamiliar urgency. I had missed her. Seeing her reminded me that there were parts of her that I loved. She poured me a tea and I sat alone at the table, quietly placing one sugar cube between my teeth and drinking. Reminded of what it was like to be cared for like this.

"This isn't the one you normally get. What's this one?" I asked her. "This one has cardamom in it," she responded. I hated the flavour of cardamom in tea, but I continued drinking, trying not to make it obvious.

"Is it good? It's very good for you. The cardamom."

"Yes, delicious."

When the tea was done, I walked into the kitchen and stood near her, leaning on the counter. I felt the urge to tell her things about my life. We'd barely spoken over the past few months. There was so much to say.

I started talking about what it had been like to meet Mahshid, to learn about queer Iranians and to simply know we exist. Her mixing got louder, the wooden spoon banging against the pot as she stirred the rice around. Her eyes darted away and she pressed her lips together, as if considering what to say. She quietly leaned over and said, "Don't talk about that stuff here. Not in front of him. You know? They don't know these things. They don't understand." I zipped up my mouth, nodded and returned to my seat.

My family environment was similar to early modern Iran, where same-sex relations weren't affirmed and recognized, but they were tolerated—so long as they existed quietly. But I didn't want to exist so quietly anymore—especially not after seeing Mahshid, who lived so fully as herself within her family. I spent the rest of that dinner seething. The instinct to be quiet had faded. If I couldn't be wholly myself with them, I didn't want to be there.

15

SPACE

The thread between my mother and me was thinning, and though I wanted distance, I wasn't immune to feeling guilty about it. Every time she called and I forwarded her to voicemail, there were the familiar pangs. They were there every time she texted me to check in, or sent along a childhood photo of me, reminiscing about old times. Or when she called to ask if she could come visit me because she'd always wanted to see the mountains out west, and because it rains and she loves the rain, and I told her, in a hurried, annoyed tone, that I was too busy.

It was easier this way. Guilt was less overwhelming than the pain of rejection. I told myself that I had to accept who my mother, and even Yara, would never be. Though I yearned to see the feminist my mother once was, the revolutionary who once protested in the streets, believing fiercely that another world was, in fact, possible. In every story she would tell, I searched for that iteration of her. In my own retellings, I crafted her in that image. I questioned whether it was delusion— imagining her as I wanted her to be, not as she was.

I remembered the conversations we had in my early twenties, when we'd talk feminism over chai, or kabobs. I told her about how the West could justify its violent wars in the Middle East— like the wars in Afghanistan or Iraq—in part by positioning the women there as oppressed and in need of saving. I quoted

Gayatri Spivak's "white men saving brown women from brown men"[6]—"Can you believe it, Mom? Like brown women need to be saved." She nodded, though one time she added that some Iranian people want to be saved by the white man, desperate for relief from a violent regime, in any form it comes. On these occasions, she would teach me something, too, about feminism and social change and revolution. Add complexity to something that felt black and white back then.

In that same conversation, I'd asked my mother when she first took off her hijab. "When I came to Canada," she responded, brief and to the point. When I probed her to share more, she remained devoid of emotion. She took her hijab off on her first day in Canada. After her interview with customs at the airport, she remembers sitting in the back of a cab with her kids, en route to a shelter. The relief of being let into the country quickly dissolving against the panic of not knowing what was to come.

I continued the scene in my mind, replaying how it must have been for her on that day of arrival. Imagined how, somewhat dissociatedly, her fingers would have slowly undone her hijab, tugging slowly and delicately at the fabric until it fell to her neck and shoulders. Briefly, she'd have thought about how disappointed her father, Baba Ali, would be. Brushing her hands through her hair, closing her eyes and focusing instead on the feeling of the wind coming from the driver's window.

"Mom, what did you feel in that moment?"

"Nothing."

"But how could that be? You wore a hijab all that time. And now you didn't have to. What did you feel?"

"Nothing."

---

6. Gayatri Spivak, "Can the Subaltern Speak?" In *Marxism and the Interpretation of Culture*, Cary Nelson, ed. (Chicago: University of Illinois Press, 1988), 296.

"Mom, why don't you just take a minute. Close your eyes and think about it."

". . . Nothing," she responded with certainty.

I rattled my brain, trying to understand how a woman fleeing a regime so oppressive to women could feel nothing in that moment. She had to have felt free, I told myself. The only thing that would make sense for her to have felt is *free*. Both of us were frustrated. Her, resisting my attempts to will a different story out of her. Me, disappointed in the story.

Since my return to Vancouver, I had descended into a deep low. Depression felt like walking in water, each step met with resistance. My research told me that routines were helpful, and so I tried to will myself into one. At seven in the evening, I would gather up my books and take the always-crowded 99 B-Line to the same coffee shop near campus. The coffee shop was much like any other—a wooden interior with as many tables as could fit, the smell of mocha and cinnamon and vanilla in the air. I started asking strangers to share their tables when there were none left, something I would have felt too shy to do before. The silver lining of feeling so little was that I also thought less of what others thought of me. Is that courage?

On a rare morning visit to the coffee shop, Nour asked to join *my* table. A mixed-race brown woman with a Muslim father, she had long dark curly hair and a round brown face. Her almond eyes were circled with dark liner, much like mine. For hours, we talked about our mutual love of creative spaces, the importance of queer community, our respective experiences of being the children of Muslim immigrants.

Two hours later, she started packing her laptop up and asked me if I wanted to go to a dispensary with her. I agreed, though I thought she said laundromat. I found it endearing to be invited to do errands with a stranger. When we got to the dispensary, I quickly realized that we were, in fact, not at a laundromat—we were at a weed shop. The dispensary was dark, and dingy, and too quiet. The scruffy bearded man at the counter led us to a back room, which then opened into another room with a pool table and old leather chairs that looked like they had been picked off a street curb. Two men were already sitting on the leather chairs, smoking what they referred to as superior shit.

"This is good shit. You ever try this?" one of the men asked us, holding out his blunt. I told them I had never tried *any* kind of marijuana, which made them encourage me more. Naturally, if I was ever going to smoke weed, I didn't think it would be here—in a random back-back-room, with strangers I was probably never going to see again. And though I was briefly reminded of what my mother would think of me, I reached for the blunt. I watched Nour take a few puffs first, breathing in, holding in and exhaling out. I imitated her as best I could before the coughing frenzy started.

A few puffs later, I erupted into uncontrollable laughter. I hadn't laughed in at least a month—not genuinely, at least. No one flinched, no one questioned what was so funny. In fact, it spread through the room quickly, all of us laughing about nothing.

Eventually, I was interrupted by one of the men trying to get my attention, asking, "You wanna go for a ride?" I stared blankly. "Hellooo . . . A ride? . . . My car is out back," he continued. I nodded and followed Nour to his car, where she quickly hopped in the front seat of the red convertible, and I got in the back. We drove through unfamiliar streets with the radio bumping the latest hip-hop tracks. Against the bass, I could barely hear the two of them talking up front, though I could see Nour's lips moving. I closed my eyes and focused on the feeling of my hair flying in the wind. The strands that gently kissed my face. *Stay with it*, I told myself. *Stay with this. What are you feeling?*

When he stopped at a red light, I had the urge to jump out of the car. Suddenly, I felt acutely aware that I was there, in a car with a complete stranger, trusting the direction of another complete stranger, headed to god-knows-where. I got the hell out. "Where are you going?" they both yelled out to me, chuckling. "I don't know," I yelled back as I weaved between cars in the oncoming traffic and finally made it to the sidewalk. I just kept walking until the streets were familiar again.

When my phone rang and the word *Mom* flashed across the screen, I muted my phone and popped it back in my coat pocket. Briefly, guilt reared its head. I got on the 99 and darted towards the most isolated window seat. The bus was unusually quiet, so I sprawled my things across two seats. I tried to focus on the feeling of being high, as if that would keep me there for longer, away from the sinking low and the guilt. I mused on how light my body felt. Like at any moment, gravity could give up on me. It could stop fighting so hard to anchor me to this earth and let me float away.

Looking up at the sky, I imagined myself floating away with my clothes billowing out like a helium balloon. The visual tickled me, and I erupted into uncontrollable laughter again. This time alone, and trying to smother my laughter with my arm, well aware of others staring at me.

16

APOLOGIES

When summer arrived, I scoured the internet in search of a new Vancouver home because I thought a change of scenery would change my mood. I didn't want one of those west-end places near the university where you rented one room—a five-by-six-metre space that would become your everything: your living room, your kitchen, your bedroom. I wanted a home. I jumped on an ad by two queer folks looking for a third roommate. A place in the east end for $400 a month sounded like a steal.

When I visited, I paused outside and mused at how much it looked like a home. The kind of place you find your average nuclear family in, with a mom gardening out back and a dad mowing the lawn. Not the kind of home I'd imagined a bunch of low-income queers in.

Philly was first to the door, introducing herself and welcoming me in. I had seen Philly before, in passing, at queer events, though I couldn't quite place her. She had distinct eyes—a dark amber brown, like maple syrup. "You can leave your shoes here," she said, pointing to the mat of shoes by the door. Her voice was the texture of cashmere. A soft, soothing tone that made you feel like everything would be okay. She waited for me to pull my shoes off and walked me into the living room, where Morgan was seated, waiting.

They stayed seated as they gestured to the seats around them. My nerves peaked again. I had never seen Morgan around the community, and when I'd asked Mahshid about them, she said they were unfamiliar to her, too. Morgan had a short pixie cut of curls and an olive-brown skin tone, similar to mine. An artistic aesthetic—their graphic liner punctuating their eyes, their paint-stained denim overalls telling the story of a humble creative. Their smile faded in and out as they spoke, their exterior cooler than Philly's.

Morgan asked deep questions that required thoughtful and nuanced responses. Like what I understood a home to be. Or my perspective on what made a good housemate. My responses were a jumble of values, politics and what I thought were the "right answers." The urgency to cloak who I was raged inside me, in favour of who I thought they wanted for the place. Like if they could smell the depression on me, they wouldn't want me.

"We have a garden," Philly said, gesturing towards the door to the back of the house. "A garden? I love gardens!" I responded enthusiastically, as if she'd said "We have cake!" Philly continued, explaining that Morgan tended to the garden and had a gift for growing vegetables. Morgan recoiled at the compliment. Perhaps there was a soft, gooey inside to this hard shell, I thought.

"How are you with cleaning?" Morgan asked. I anxiously muttered on about how I was a clean roommate, and that I preferred schedules and co-cleaning. The words poured out of my mouth faster than my brain could process the question. Even if I had taken a moment to think, explaining that I could barely get out of bed these days felt embarrassing. No matter how kind and warm you were, few people seemed to be interested in living with someone who was either avoiding cleaning or cleaning in random, hyper-focused spurts.

A few days later, Philly called me with an invitation to move in, though there was one caveat. Morgan wanted the option of asking me to leave if it didn't go well in the first month. Though the idea of being asked to leave a month in was unsettling, I said yes.

Up the creaky pull-down steps was my new space: a cozy attic. Small spaces were easy because I owned so little: one suitcase worth of clothes and a backpack of books. Most of the room was taken up by a twin-size bed and antique-looking wooden chest. On the left was just enough room for a dresser. A small window overlooked the mountains; on sunny mornings, it would wake me with the most gorgeous stream of light. Next to it, a small vintage-looking mirror. The last roommate had taped a little baggie with a small joint to the back of it, with a handwritten note that said, *I hope this room is good to you*.

The first few weeks, especially, I stayed in my room a lot. I was anxious of what the others thought of me, every interaction bearing the heavy weight of whether I would be welcome to stay or asked to go. Would it be because I said something wrong or because I, for whatever reason, just didn't fit with them? Not knowing by what criteria I would be judged was overwhelming. So instead, I turtled away in that attic room.

At night, a restlessness overcame me. Often the others would sit quietly in the living room, cozy on the couch, opening up a new book or working on a new project. I thought about calling Mom to tell her I could see the mountains from my tiny little attic window, except I wouldn't tell her I lived in an attic because she would worry about how warm it could possibly be in an attic room. I would tell her that since moving, I thought about her when it rained, which is to say I thought about her a lot those days. Except I didn't want to tell her that because she'd ask me if I had an umbrella, and I'd have to say I kept losing my umbrellas on the buses, and she'd worry. She'd think about me and want to call me, and I didn't want her to think about me, so instead, I would leave the attic room for a coffee shop, where my thoughts were briefly quieted.

Coffee shops had continued to be a beloved ritual. In the daytime, there was always an eclectic group of people—different from hour to hour, day to day. But at night, there was cohesion. You would generally see the same characters at any given place. This time, I had started frequenting a new coffee shop downtown, thirty minutes from my new place. A late-night spot where university students would stay up studying, buzzed on coffee they'd refill every three hours. I'd sit at the same long table with the same three men, who I would learn were studying finance. Eventually, we would say a few words to each other, but mostly, we studied quietly next to one another.

At one o'clock in the morning, I considered packing my things up. By two, I finally negotiated taking myself home. I'd take the bus back to the main street, which was always a gamble because you wouldn't know who would be on the bus at two o'clock in the morning. Sometimes, it was quiet—me and a few students from the coffee shop or a few unhoused folks seeking warmth. Sometimes, it was rowdier. Drunk men would stare and slowly find their way closer and closer to my seat— always leaving me alone once I hopped off the bus to walk the fifteen minutes to the house. I would say *"Bismallah"* on my solo late-night walks, as my mother taught me to when I needed blessings and protection.

Eventually, my roommates started to notice and comment on my late-night solo travels. One morning, I entered the kitchen in my pyjamas at half past eleven, ready to steep some black tea before class. Philly and Morgan had already started their days and were filling up their own mugs with coffee and tea.

"Whoop, sorry! Just sliding by." I smiled, trying to exude as much warmth as I could muster while I reached between them for a tea bag from the jar. "Must . . . have . . . coffee," I chuckled.

"You got home pretty late. What time was it?" Morgan asked me with equal parts curiosity and concern.

"Yeah, how late were you out?" Philly chimed in.

"Oh, I was working at that coffee shop until around one or two in the morning. Got home a bit after that."

"That's really late. How'd you get home?"

"I took the bus and then I walked."

"That's really late to be walking alone. There's not much light up from the main street."

It had been a while since anyone had noticed my where-abouts, and their noticing was unsettling for me. I struggled to trust the intentions behind it, to divorce it from surveillance. I tried to remind myself that they likely asked because I was part of their home, because we were building relationships and because they cared about my safety. Yet I couldn't shake the urge to withdraw, and retreat into my room. So much so that I gradually stopped my coffee shop visits.

When October came around, the two threw around the idea of a harvest celebration. By then, Morgan had already spoken to me twice about my cleaning shortcomings. The dishes, which were to be cleaned within twenty-four hours (and, among them, the cast-iron pan, which was not to be soaked in water). And the front door, which was not a place to forget your bag for days.

Their asks awoke an anxiety in me that felt impossible to tame. I far preferred the depression to whatever beast this was. Tense and on edge, I worried that the third warning would have me out, looking for a new place. Besides, that my cleaning was a problem at all was embarrassing enough. If I had felt the need to retreat before, the urge was now to shoot myself to the moon.

The idea of a harvest celebration sounded nice in theory, but it would require me to be in the same room as them and not on the moon. Nonetheless, I could see their excitement. Part of me wanted to feel like I was "one of them," too.

Each roommate was allowed to bring up to four people, and so I chose Mahshid. I studied the email the two sent out, which included a long list of things we needed to refrain from: no nuts, no nut oils, no scents, no pineapple, no lime, no shell-fish, no citrus, no pork.

The day of, Morgan asked to borrow my new eyeshadow palette from MAC and it felt like progress. That we could bond over makeup was a hopeful opening. The MAC palette was a luxury purchase I could barely afford. Four autumn colours—two that lay on my eyes with a velvety, glittery brown. When they returned it to me, they told me the palette wasn't as good as their own palettes and the colour payoff was poor. What I wanted to say was that you needed a primer to make the colours pop; otherwise, it looked faded. Instead, I instinctually agreed. Again, the words just fell out of my mouth around Morgan, before my mouth could consult my brain.

Dinner was a beautiful spread centred around a roast turkey, basted to perfection. Around it, casseroles, fried vegetables, salads and bread. The living room was crowded with everyone's beloved friends, each person distracted by the delicious food. I was grateful to be sitting next to Mahshid, who joked that there was never enough food at these things. Her humour a fleeting break from my brain, which had already started planning how I would clean the place afterwards.

When everyone left and the others went to bed, I stayed up until three in the morning, cleaning everything I could. I googled how to clean the cast iron and followed the instructions I had already forgotten from Morgan. I washed the pans, and dishes, and cutlery until they were spotless and put away. Moved the furniture to the usual spots. And in the end, I hoped that it would be enough.

In the morning, Morgan and Philly remarked on how clean everything was, thanking me for it. It felt good to finally get something right in this home. "I'm sorry—I wish I could've done more," I responded like the aunties I'd grown up with, who had used those exact words. After that comment, it seemed that Morgan was more distant with me. The warmer I was, the more they pulled away in conversations until our interactions became shorter and shorter.

The evening Morgan approached me to talk, I felt both relief that the sudden coldness wasn't in my mind, and dread. Their flat affect offered me no solace.

"Do you notice how much you apologize?" They paused and looked at me, their undertone of judgment making me want to unzip my skin like a literal meat suit and hide under the couch. They reassured me that while my cleaning had greatly improved, my apologizing was the issue now. "It's a lot. You apologize a lot," they explained. The words *a lot* felt sharp, slicing across my quick-beating heart. My whole body froze, awaiting the next blow. "Do you wonder why that is?" They went on to explain that while I was smart and strong in other ways, my apologies made me seem small and meek, helpless almost.

Small. I rolled my tongue over the word. *Small.* The more I repeated the word, the more heated I felt. *Small.* Like I wanted to smash the word against the pavement into a thousand pieces and show them just how un-small I was. I took a breath in and with the firmest voice I could muster said: "I don't think I apologize a lot, and no one has ever said that they feel I apologize too much."

"You apologize when you're trying to pass by someone. You apologize when someone bumps into you, even when it's not your fault. You even said 'I'm sorry for not doing enough' after having cleaned the whole night after our Friendsgiving dinner. It's a lot," they repeated. Seeing that we were both unmovable, Morgan went upstairs.

In the morning, I lay awake in bed, googling variations of "women apologizing too much." I had seen these articles before, floating on social media, and been mostly unbothered by them. They were the perspectives of largely white feminists who believed women were socialized to apologize for everything under the sun—including their mere existence—and that apologizing less would get us ahead.

Were there moments when I apologized and really didn't need to? Sure, but that didn't mean it was a problem. Instead, I kept researching, collecting proof for why this part of me had meaning and value, as if it would change Morgan's perspective.

Perhaps I held on tightly to my apologies because I saw so much of my mother, my culture in them. As I lay in bed, I remembered when we travelled to Iran and my mother unpacked her bags, handing each of my family members their souvenirs. "I'm sorry I didn't bring more," she said with a smile that warmed the room. The others in the room responded with equal parts tenderness and charm. "You coming is enough," one said. "You are the gift, Khaleh," another said. Suddenly, the room felt like it had been gently kissed on the forehead. An apology could do that—change the spirit of a whole room.

I'd felt so proud of mastering these nuanced expressions, or what one might call the Persian art of etiquette, during my last visit to Iran. When I had been offered the front seat of the car, I declined, aware of our *tarof* principles, where you say no multiple times before it's okay to say yes. When I'd finally accepted the front seat, I turned back towards my Khaleh Soraya, who was sitting behind me with my mom, and said: "I'm sorry my back is to you, Auntie." "A flower has no front or back," she'd responded.

The artful practice of the apology didn't seem to translate beyond borders. To Western feminists, the nuance was lost in favour of a more monolithic portrayal of women apologizing as symbolic of internalized patriarchy and misogyny.

That day, I took the bus over to Mahshid's house, thinking about whether or not to tell her about all this. My puffy eyes gave it away before I could speak. She knew something was wrong. I walked over to the cabinet in the kitchen, pulled out the big container of sour keys and popped one in my mouth.

"Oh, friend—what's happened?" she asked.

"It's something Morgan told me," I said. Immediately, the tears started pouring from my eyes. Taking short breaths in, I asked: "Do you think I apologize too much?"

Mahshid immediately said, "No, they're just being a real jerk to you. And if even you did, you still wouldn't need to change it."

"She gave the example of my apologizing for not doing enough after cleaning . . ."

"But that's just what we say. We're Persians!" she exclaimed. We both laughed.

"I haven't been able to sleep. The house is so hostile."

"Go." She gestured towards her bedroom. "You need sleep." And I did.

Two months later, in the wee hours of the night, Mahshid and I finagled my mattress down the attic steps and into a U-Haul.

Mahshid drove me to a new place I had rented temporarily while I decided what to do next.

In the quiet of my new room—one mattress on the ground, one suitcase and one backpack—I sobbed. Leaving that house had granted me enough clarity to realize it was never about the apologizing—not directly, at least. I had left Toronto believing that I could feel more free here. Like if only I could get enough distance from my mother's gaze, I could be my whole self. Except leaving hadn't made me feel free, any more than my mother's leaving Iran had made her feel free.

There was always someone else's gaze that I worried about. Here, it was Morgan's. In Toronto, it was my sister's and mother's. I was constantly shape-shifting into what I thought others wanted me to be, vying for their acceptance. It never seemed to be enough, anyway. Here, apologizing less would be one more thing I'd change about myself, not for me but for someone else. If I was to ever feel more liberated, I had to reckon with what kept me captive: my overwhelming fear of rejection.

I spent days crying in that room. It was as if a dam had broken and I was floating in an ocean of grief. And the more I floated in it, the more I thought of my mother and missed her. All that sadness was carrying me downstream—towards home, in Toronto. And though the wounds of rejection were fresh, I wanted to know what it would be like to be my whole self around Mom. More so, I wanted to know that I could do it.

When I saw Mahshid next, I reluctantly told her the news. "It's time for me to go," I said, tears already welling up.

She looked at me knowingly. "No," she said, half joking.

"I'll come back," I promised her.

"Everyone always says that and they don't come back," she responded.

"It won't be like the others who never come back. I will," I said.

At the end of the summer, having finished my graduate degree, I packed my suitcase and left to stay with Yara. It was an act of faith: returning home without knowing whether things would be better—but believing in the possibility of it.

17

MOURN

"She's just like you—*Zaynab*," Mom said to me, referring to Dory, my four-year-old niece, who was a sensitive soul. Yara and her husband, Dan, had invited me to live with them while I pursued a social work degree in Kitchener. Mom now lived down the street, visiting every couple of days. And I was on a new journey with all of them, trying to be more open about my queerness.

"Sensitive!" Mom continued, trying not to laugh while Dory pouted and argued about the unfairness of not getting to wear a tutu out in public.

Zaynab is a not-so-endearing term amongst some Iranians for someone who is prone to expressions of sadness. It's a reference to Zaynab bint Ali, the daughter of Fatimah bint Muhammad and Ali ibn Abi Talib, and the granddaughter of the Prophet Muhammad. When I asked Mom why *Zaynab* specifically, her response was "Because she cried a lot," which felt woefully insufficient when I learned who she was.

During the Battle of Karbala in 680 CE, many of her relatives were massacred by the Umayyad Caliph Yazid I, including her two sons and her brother, Imam Husayn, who had chosen to resist Yazid's tyrannical leadership. Amongst Shia Muslims, Imam Husayn is known as a martyr who sacrificed himself for truth, justice and righteousness.

The tears my mother was referencing came from Zaynab's grief following the loss of her family members in the Battle of Karbala. Amidst the loss, Zaynab and other women and children became prisoners of Yazid. What my mother never shared was that Zaynab delivered a sermon in the court of Yazid that was so powerful it continues to be repeated and studied today. Speaking with conviction and bravery, she pointed to the oppression and injustices of Yazid and the battle, moving others to such empathy that eventually they were all released. Zaynab is now known widely for speaking truth to power and is seen by many as an iconic feminist figure in Muslim history. She symbolizes courage, strength and sacrifice.

The battle is annually commemorated on Ashura, a day of mourning for Imam Husayn. The last time I was in Iran, I happened to be there on this day. "What's that sound?" I'd asked, hearing chants and loud, drum-like thuds. "It's Ashura. They're beating their chests," Mom responded. I listened closely, realizing it *was* the sound of people beating their chests. "But . . . why?" I asked. Mourning was a deeply spiritual practice, I learned; it honoured Imam Husayn *and* what he represents—the ongoing struggle against oppression and injustice.

Knowing this history, every time Mom called me—and now Dory—Zaynab, I reminded myself that Zaynab was a powerful figure who honoured her own grief. I couldn't help but wonder why my mother had minimized her to merely her tears, as if expressing sadness over the loss of family—let alone any loss—was "dramatic." Especially knowing the persistent ache of losing her own brother, Shahin.

I wondered if someone had called Mom Zaynab as a child, too. "*Stop*," I told her, feeling suddenly protective of Dory. A word that I had heard both Yasaman and Yara say before, but rarely myself with Mom. Dory was at an age where there was no armour yet; there were no instincts to suppress, repress, minimize or avoid. There were just big, big feelings and the impulse to express them. I felt protective of that. *Let her feel this*, I thought.

Having seen my parents' marriage fall apart, I was well aware that sometimes you don't return to people or places. There's just too much wreckage and rubble behind you to look back. If you're lucky, the wreckage becomes a beautiful ruin, worth revisiting. Like how Persepolis is still marvelled at by tourists who stand before it, imagining what once lived in the palace complex, before so much of it was looted and destroyed by Alexander the Great.

Returning to Kitchener-Waterloo for school, I was hopeful that what was once wreckage would become a beautiful ruin. I landed in Laurier's social work program and found myself in a sea of mostly white women with no more than seven people of colour in my classes. I wasn't surprised by this, given my previous experience at the university, but I felt different this time. More self-assured as I walked through the hallways, shoulders squared and eyes gazing straight ahead. The instinct was to take up space, to speak my truth, even if it made others uncomfortable. It's not that I wasn't speaking truthfully before; it's that I'd mostly done so in spaces where truth was already acceptable, echoed by those around me, like in feminist circles. Though I know now that the kind of safety I felt in those groups was certainly not generalizable to all feminist spaces, nor to all who join those spheres.

Being back in the city made me think about Ren again. Months before, while still in Vancouver, I had sent them a message on social media, anticipating my return to the city they still lived in. I apologized for having broken up with them when I was in Iran. For never giving them closure, even when they begged. It was a cruel way to end things. In the letter,

I said I hoped we could meet in person. Any inner hesitation I felt was countered by a relentless desire to see their face again. I still saw beauty in what we'd shared.

I was still commuting from Yara's in Thornhill, so I drove an hour and a half to visit them in Kitchener at the Yeti, a dreamy hipster café with a green chalkboard wall behind the cash register, bright-red splashes of colour and a vegan menu. Ren was vegan now. Having gotten there twenty minutes early, I ruminated on all the ways I could say *I'm sorry*. In my family, there were no road maps for returning to ruptures and repairing. You just you moved on.

Ren arrived late, walking over to me with the same gentle smile they'd offered in that fourth-year gender studies class years ago. My heart still fluttered seeing them walk towards me. Beneath their toque, I could see their freshly shaven head. New tattoos mapped their arms, completing the sleeve they'd always wanted. They were queerer now, if that was even possible. We smiled at each other at first, allowing a moment of silence, as if we were tracing each other's faces, confirming that this surreal moment of meeting was, in fact, real.

Ren and I had never been much for simple pleasantries. We both acknowledged that we never thought we'd return to each other again. And as always, we dove deep right away. Perhaps that was what I loved most about us—we would plunge into the depths together, even if we couldn't see the ocean floor, or our feet.

Apologies came oozing out of me. I needed them to know that I really did love them. That the ending was never about them. In ways, it felt like I had sacrificed Ren for my own comfort, my own illusion of peace.

What was more important to Ren was knowing the truth. "What happened?" they asked, referring to the period when I went to Iran.

I hesitated. The idea of having to return to those memories made my stomach turn. I was repulsed by the version of me that would have married a man and moved to Iran, all to avoid confronting and accepting my queerness. I pushed through the rumblings of nausea and told them the truth.

I took as deep a breath in as I could muster and explained that going back home to Iran had left me with unbearable anguish over my queerness, over having to choose between one identity and another, belonging and selfhood. I had been sure that coming out would mean losing my family, and ultimately, never being able to return home again. The agony of that had deepened each day, until eventually I broke up with Ren *and* my queer self. I'd told myself that no one would ever know that I was queer—except my mother and Yara, who would easily never speak about it again, if they could.

After a brief pause, I looked up at Ren, whose warm gaze enveloped me like a hug. "I figured that's what happened," they said. Not with disdain or judgment, as I'd expected, but with compassion. There was something earth-shifting about telling Ren the truth and seeing their kind, compassionate eyes looking back at me. I was realizing that some of us spend years alone with a narrative, absolutely shitting on ourselves, and not realizing that perhaps others have moved on and it's you who hasn't.

As I integrated back into Kitchener-Waterloo, there was a growing desire to see Ren again. I had just moved back—part-time at least—to be closer to the school. I invited them to casually hang out, not knowing what the desire was and where it came from. This time, we met at Jill's, an uptown bar that appeared to be struggling with its identity. Small and dark, supposedly retro, with orange walls, dangling holiday lights and art you'd find in a dorm room.

They walked in with a warm smile again, smoothly sliding onto the chair across me. They were still small and thin, though their hair had grown back. It was softer now, less bleached and straightened. As we began talking, their voice softened along with their facial expressions. "Yeah . . . uhh . . . good, I've been . . . good." They were never one for flow. Words fell out of their mouth like Jenga blocks. One on top of the other, and sometimes all of it crashing down at once.

Ren told me excitedly that they were poly now, and in a relationship with an academic who sounded intimidatingly smart. They were living in Kitchener in a home with two pups, a bunch of plants and beloved community surrounding them. They had a car, too, which felt very adult, even though they were still trying to figure out their career. I felt a hint of jealousy as I imagined what could've been if I had never left.

By the winter, I'd asked Ren if they'd be willing to go on a date with me. The more time I spent in the city, the more I yearned to be closer to Ren. When their name popped up on my phone, it felt like the same thrill of sitting near them in class, reading the tattoos on their arms.

We met at a restaurant at the local museum. Though I had never been there, I had passed by its windows several times. The inside looked cozy, with warm mood lighting, a lot of wood and grown-ups holding upscale cocktails. I wanted something that oozed maturity. Perhaps I wanted to "woo" them. Or to remind myself that we weren't those twenty-somethings anymore.

Ren walked through the doors, and there was a swirling inside me, a gentle gasp. I was abundantly aware that this time felt so different than the last. There were no parts of me that wanted to recoil or hide in the darkness of a sweaty club. I sat across from them with my head resting on my left hand, swooning openly with my beaming eyes focused on only them. My body upright and leaning forward—not collapsed, or small, as I once was. I felt sure who of I was and comfortable living in that truth.

Our conversations always seemed to return to the same thing. Us, sharing memories of old times, like we were at a celebration of life, reminiscing about everything from the mundane to the silly to the terrible.

"Do you remember that time with the bedbugs?"

"When we slept in my car?"

We both burst out laughing. In the dead of winter, Ren had become convinced that they had bedbugs at their apartment, so we'd spent hours packing their clothes and bedsheets into garbage bags, to be cleaned. Until the whole thing was sorted out, they were going to stay with me. The first morning after staying at my apartment, we both woke up in a panic, obsessively scratching our skin until it felt like everything and everywhere was bitten. Though there were no bumps, we hunted for proof, flipping the mattress and convincing ourselves that the few spots we saw were definitely bedbugs.

Neither of us could shake the feeling that we were sleeping on bugs that next night, imagining those little fuckers biting our skin. With only our coats and mitts on, we tried sleeping in my mom's car instead. Spent most of the night awake, shaking from the bitter cold. The next day, the landlord had someone inspect the room and confirm that there were definitely no bedbugs—just our vivid imaginations.

The more memories we shared, the more I realized that there was a sort of amnesia I'd developed around the harder moments of our relationship. Like the time we went to a concert for my birthday and Ren disappeared into the crowd behind me to smoke weed with a stranger. Or the drunken argument after Ren, while performing drag, fished a five-dollar bill out of their ex-partner's mouth. Or how often I would turn to Ren and whisper, "Everyone is looking at you," uncomfortable with their hyper-visibility. Or, more to the point, how visible they made me.

In ways, it felt similar to my mother's purified stories of Shahin. I recalled how her grief had thinned the line between man and myth so much that even she wasn't sure what was real and what was story. I wondered if I had done the same. Turned Ren into a myth—a sacred figure who was once sacrificed and, now, who I worshipped at the altar of.

That night, the truth gently seeped in, revealing the cracks in my illusion. Though our relationship was beautiful in many ways, it wasn't the idyllic romance I'd been imagining. There were issues of jealousy and rage that had eroded our connection. Yet the more the truth seeped in, the more I wanted to tape my illusion back together with hyper-romantic gestures, like lavish dinners and promises of getaways.

The next weekend, Ren abruptly ended things in a text message. They softly explained that though it was lovely to reconnect, there was too much anxiety and worry present for them. And that really was the end. While it was a devastating ending, it wasn't cruel.

I stayed in bed all day, trying to piece together what this experience meant, because I desperately wanted it to *mean* something. I'd been so sure that I was returning to the site of a wound and healing it, like I could get it "right" this time. I was returning to the beginning, I'd thought, where we could start again. Instead, it was a pilgrimage back to three years before, where we'd ended off. My twenty-one-year-old self waiting, as if knowing that one day I would return to grieve with her. And now, with the finality of its ending, I felt compelled to mourn: to fold over and cry out in gut-wrenching agony. "Let yourself feel this," I told myself as tears poured out of me.

I recalled that twenty-one-year-old self who carried her body weight in shame, self-loathing and disgust. Reflected deeply on the internal battle of that time that had ensued between the freedom-loving, truth-seeking parts of me and the fearful parts that preferred to stay in the dark, or inside the box. The curious parts of me that sought desire beyond the bounds of heteronormativity and the parts of me that folded in fear. The parts who danced so freely at Club Renaissance, tracing Ren's body against my fingers, and the parts who couldn't even hold their hand.

In ways, I finally understood why people *wanted* to mourn, as I'd asked my mother all those years ago during Ashura. Here, mourning was a way to honour the loss of our relationship, its sacredness. Sacred, in the way love is *always* sacred. Sacred, in its commitment to truth—however painful and uncomfortable it was for the younger me to discover and live in it.

In the two years I would spend in Kitchener-Waterloo, I would still see them in passing. Our brief conversations no less warm and kind than before. The butterflies still alive and fluttering. I felt immense gratitude for having loved and been loved by them. There were no regrets in having returned; what was once wreckage had indeed become a beautiful ruin to me. One that was equal parts exquisite and devastating. And above all, I learned something new about love, too. That not all love stories end in togetherness; but still, they are love stories—worth honouring with as much care and compassion as one can muster.

18

REPRIEVE

The social work internship I snagged with a Toronto-area school board felt like a dream gig—I'd be working with queer and trans youth who had figured so much of themselves out long before I had. Partway through the term, it was tradition to have all the staff and interns share stories about themselves with all the students. One by one, each of us sat on a single chair at the front of the room, thirty students staring at us patiently. I thought about what story I would tell.

The story, as I told it, began with twenty-year-old me spotting Ren in that gender studies class, the tattoo on the back of their arm pulling me in. Firmly, I named the blended identities I held—that I'm a queer Muslim woman from an immigrant family, who grew up in the suburbs of Toronto. Their faces lit up as I talked about my first love, or when I named an identity that they too shared. For the first time, I told that story not with shame, fear or hesitation, but with unapologetic joy. Their twinkling eyes telling me a story so different than the one I had told myself for so long. Here, I didn't feel cheated out of my first love. I felt lucky to have had a love so big, so transformative, with a person I still knew and adored, years later.

It felt like a stroke of luck that had landed me here, or even an act of mercy from the universe. My first internship was on a crisis team where I mostly sat in a back room, reading course work and finishing my essays, minimally interacting with humans. I wasn't above begging the program coordinators for another placement, and my begging paid off. I was an asset in this school; I could see it in the bright, responsive faces of the students.

Another intern, Amelia, had started before me, and I worried that we'd be in competition, each trying to be the smarter, more experienced student. When I met her, the thought seemed comical. On the first day, she asked to catch a ride with me from one of the schools to the main office, and within five minutes, we were belting out Camila Cabello's "Havana" and deconstructing professionalism with our shimmying shoulders.

Amelia could only be described as a home with the front doors unlocked, the windows wide open, an unkempt front lawn, a fresh pie on the porch and no security system. Inviting, warm, exhilarating and sometimes concerning. Having moved here from Newfoundland, she often broke into her mother's accent, which was just as endearing as my own mother's accent. She said things like "Jesus, Mary and Joseph!" and called her friends "b'ys." Perhaps the most profound connection between Amelia and me was her love of home. "There's no ocean here. I miss the ocean," she would say to me when we drove past the lakeshore. Her yearning reminded me of my own. I wondered if she ached for the ocean the way I ached for the afternoon chai, the apricots, the warmth of my aunties' hugs.

When I dropped her off at her house one day, she told me that I was "very Toronto" when I drove. "Toronto" wasn't an identity I felt very connected to, especially having grown up in the suburbs. But being cut off by cars, especially luxury vehicles, brought out an anger in me that rarely reared its head. I liked to think of it as the Marxism running in my blood, from my late

Dayee Shahin. I felt no qualms about cursing at the upper middle class of the city, especially from the inside of my car, where they couldn't hear me. "What the fuck is your problem, ASSHOLE!" I yelled out, my hands shaking in the air. Amelia laughed and reminisced about how no one back home drove the way people here drove, and certainly no one cursed others out and raged the way we did. A comment like that would usually spiral me into shame; I far preferred to be seen as soft and gentle than aggressive and angry. But her playfulness made me feel like it was okay to be messy—both/and.

Where Amelia seemed to be running towards home, I was running away. I had moved back in with Yara for three reasons. One, there were better internships in Toronto. Two, cockroaches had infiltrated the kitchen in my Kitchener apartment. Three, I had a mountain of debt from student loans, and Yara and Dan were generous enough to let me stay with them rent-free.

Yara's house was further north of the city now and was enormous compared to where we'd once lived. She had "made it"—if making it meant far surpassing the financial and housing insecurity we'd grown up with. Inside, her house was eerily bare—white walls, a lavish couch and a dining table, but not much else.

Since I'd returned to her house, I'd noticed that Yara had increasingly made a home of her couch. Her body tucked underneath a blanket, a bag of Doritos next to her and a bowl of yogurt. Her fingers searching her hair for coarse strands that she would glide over repeatedly until they pulled out from their roots. The quiet of the home only interrupted by the crunching of chips. Yara had gone through multiple failed fertility cycles and collapsed into a deep low. When I'd pull on my coat and tell her I was going Amelia's, she often said nothing. I repeated myself two, three times some nights until she turned her head towards me and nodded. It never felt like she was ignoring me; it felt like she was far away, in another world inside of herself.

When she seemed lighter, I would test the waters to see if she was open to talking about my queerness, which we hadn't discussed since I originally came out to her. I would drop a fact about queer people, or talk about an essay on queerness and ask her what she thought, but she barely responded. I took it as confirmation that she was no closer. Though disappointed, I tried to have other conversations with her, too; the response was just as minimal. The only thing we could reliably talk about was Dory, whose quirkiness eased the tension and brought us together. Like the many nights she would storm into my room after showering, to rub her bare butt on my bedsheets, laughing uncontrollably as my sister yelled, "Dory, get back here!" We could laugh about that, at least, Yara and I.

Before I met Amelia, reprieve was found by driving myself down to the queer community centre in the Church-Wellesley Village, where I would park and stay in my car. Though I wanted to go in, the vulnerability felt too scary. Instead, I turned off the engine, pushed the seat back and observed the busy street. The queer people sitting on the steps of the building, huddled together under a blanket. The queer couples and friends, hand in hand, walking down Church Street towards the neon lights and gay bars. Thirty minutes later, I would drive back home.

Amelia's home became my warm escape from Yara's. A basement apartment in the west end with a single room and the tiniest kitchen I had ever seen. You could measure the place in steps. Five steps from bed to fridge, three steps from fridge to stairs out, six steps from bed to washroom. The outside world ceased to exist when you climbed down the steps into her apartment.

After work, I would change into her spare pyjamas and snuggle in next to her in bed, and we would talk about our lives, supporting each other with our anxieties and stresses. Or we'd snuggle under her sheets, watching romantic comedies and eating a box of Krispy Kreme donuts. It was an intimacy I had never felt before with a friend. One that reminded me of the sisterhood *sighehs* in pre-modern and early modern Iran, where women would court other women for companionship, spending time together and, later, exchanging vows. Our relationship was one that felt romantic at times, and platonic at others. One that redefined what I understood friendship to mean. In the middle of all the ugly and hard, there was this beautiful thing with Amelia.

The more time I spent with Amelia, the more it felt like she—a white woman from Newfoundland—was more cultured than I was. She would share stories about mummering, a Christmas tradition where groups of people would show up to houses in their neighbourhood, disguised in all kinds of costumes. Or being screeched in—a ceremony where non-Newfoundlanders became "honorary Newfoundlanders," taking a shot of the potent dark rum called screech, kissing a cod and reciting an old saying. Her stories brought to the surface how disconnected I'd come to feel from my own culture, making me wish I had my own traditions and rituals to share.

Before the divorce, Mom had become more devoutly Muslim than I'd ever seen her. She was living in Iran for six months at a time with Ehsan, wearing her hijab diligently, praying five times a day and reading the Quran. Even Yara was more Muslim than me, reading her Quran every night and wearing a verse around her neck.

What I missed most was going to a *sofreh-e nazri*—the Muslim gathering amongst women that centred around food and prayer, a ritual that had brought me great comfort as a child. How we'd sit side by side, leaning into any feeling that emerged from our spirits. The symphony of sounds that emerged—one's heart being gently drummed upon, the singing of prayers, the hum of crying. I missed how spiritually nourished I felt by the end. Lighter, even.

The memory of the sofreh sparked as eagerness to return to Muslim traditions and practices, and I sought out a queer-inclusive mosque. It presented an opportunity to connect with Islam on my terms—not from a place of fear, but from a place of curiosity and even hope. The Jummah prayer was happening at the same community centre where I had parked before— my place of temporary reprieve. This time, I was going in.

I spent an hour finding the right clothes to wear, panicking about what, in my closet, felt modest enough for this. Finally, I settled on a black hijab, blouse and wide-legged pants. Nervously, I walked upstairs and towards the room where I saw El-Farouk Khaki, one of the mosque's co-founders, warmly welcoming people in. I joined the circle and waited nervously for it all to begin, not knowing what to expect. El-Farouk started with a few notes about the space, including a statement on modesty, expressing that you were free to define modesty as you liked, and to dress as you liked in the space. Immediately, I could breathe, my nerves dissipating.

I followed the prayer ritual with the others until, slowly, parts returned to me, like body memory. For a moment, I was flooded with memories of Baba Ali praying at dawn, his booming voice waking me up. I kissed my forehead to the ground and imagined my Khaleh's face, teaching me how to pray, heart-warmed by my enthusiasm.

After leaving, I felt so moved by it all, I spent twenty minutes sobbing in my car. It was like hearing the *Azaan*, the Islamic call to prayer, for the first time in the streets of Iran as a child—heart-stoppingly beautiful. When the tears passed, there was an emerging excitement in me, an eagerness to redefine Muslimness in ways that honoured *all* of my identities. I thought about twenty-one-year-old me, who never could have imagined this. That our queerness could belong in the same room as our Muslim identity, neither one being hidden or exiled.

I wanted to tell my mother about it all, so I visited her apartment—the one she had previously lived in with her now ex-husband, Ehsan. We hadn't talked about her reasons for divorcing him. She had been tight-lipped every time I probed. Sitting crossed-legged on the couch, she handed a cup of steeped tea with sugar cubes over to me. Making herself comfortable, she shared that living in Iran had illuminated how different she was now, having lived in Canada for decades. First, she noted dramatically, without consistent internet, she'd felt like she was dying. Second, she was troubled by the conservative beliefs of others. While the younger generations were more progressive, many of the elders she knew still carried conservative Islamic beliefs about women's roles in the family, etiquette and modesty. This was interesting, particularly because I never saw her interrupt those beliefs in Iran, and so I'd presumed she agreed—at least in part.

"But I thought you enjoyed being more devoutly Muslim?" I asked her. It turned out her turn towards devout practice had been more about survival than personal desire. The more she stayed in Iran, the more she struggled to define Muslimness for herself. How could she reconcile the Islam she had believed in during the seventies—something that felt radically compassionate and hopeful—with what she was witnessing now in Iran:

the government's crackdowns on free speech, the mass poverty, the overall lack of agency? Though she was still Muslim, her experiences in Iran left her feeling painfully mixed about her faith and regretful that the Revolution had led to this.

I thought hearing about a queer-inclusive mosque might remind her of the Islam she once knew. Enthusiastically, I told her about the Jummah prayer I had been to, where modesty was self-defined and all genders sat side by side. A familiar expression flashed across her face, reminding me of my early university years when I tried to tell her about my feminist organizing. A face full of hesitation that said, "Don't get too involved in this kind of thing."

Instead of moving on, I asked her point-blank, "Do you think it's possible to be queer and Muslim, Mom?" She responded that "they," meaning more conservative Muslims, would never say you could be both. "But what do *you* believe?" I asked again, emphasizing that I wanted *her* understanding. She paused before quietly saying, "Sure," still with hesitation in her face. She quickly collected the tea and sugar cubes and walked back to the kitchen. It felt like avoidance, but I reminded myself that there was acknowledgement here—that a step was a step, no matter how much hesitation and discomfort it came with.

While Mom was turning away from Islam, I was turning towards it, even running towards it, with renewed hope.

19

ARRIVALS

The story of how my parents left Iran for Canada was a clean, familiar one, about hope and opportunity. The desire for a safe upbringing for their daughters made sense to me. But the narrative incongruities that I'd intuited as a child became more glaring as I grew older. The true story, which Mom didn't tell me until I was in my thirties, is messy—but it's aligned with what I know of my parents now, and what I've grown to understand about the grief she holds.

In September of 1990 in Esfahan, my father came home with one-way bus tickets to Turkey for a family vacation. Mom enthusiastically packed one suitcase for Dad, herself, Yara and Yasaman, leaving room for gifts and goods to bring back. Istanbul was a dreamland to my mother. Its beautiful historic scenery, the busy streets, the smell of donair. They stayed at a delightful four-star hotel and visited the bazaars, the fruit markets, the modern clothing stores, the restaurants and all the common tourist attractions. When the excitement of new adventure wore off, though, an anxious pit began to grow in Mom's stomach. The gnawing realization that it had been ten days since she'd spoken to her mother, who she was sure would be worrying at this point.

After she made numerous attempts to find out when they were going home, my father finally responded: "We are never going back." He delivered the blow bluntly, nothing to soften the words. Panicked, Mom responded: "What? What about our life, our home, our things?"

"You have nothing there anymore. No furniture, no belongings, nothing. From here, we're going to Canada."

Stunned, Mom tried everything that day. She pleaded with him. She pleaded with God. She bartered. She begged. She prayed. And when nothing worked, he finally said: "If you want to go back, go. I'm not coming with you." So she packed her bags, got on a bus with Yara and Yasaman, and returned home alone.

Their little apartment in Esfahan held so many things that were dear to her. It held her couches, the coffee table, a Persian rug, the glass cabinet with her china set, a few photographs of family, a tiny television set. It was in this apartment that she'd learned to cook after my father had purchased a book of recipes for her. She sat with that book, reading and practising every day, until she perfected her *gheimeh*.

There wasn't much to her home, but she loved it. There was no beautiful garden, no fig trees, no rose bushes. There was a huge balcony and two bedrooms, though—enough for a family of four and their simple belongings.

When Mom returned to the apartment with Yasaman and Yara, she found the hollowed-out shell of the home she once treasured. The emptiness was enough to dizzy her. As she walked through the rooms, her stomach twisted and turned. She bit her lips to keep the building agony inside her, away from the kids. There was no tiny television set, no rug, no glass cabinet, no clothes, no photographs, no dinnerware. There was nothing here, she realized. He had really left her with nothing to come back to.

She picked up the phone and called Amou Javid, knowing he was the softest of my father's five brothers. "Please," she pleaded, "please bring me back my home." Stoic and matter-of-fact, he explained that my father had given direct orders to each of the brothers and sisters to keep her belongings locked away from her.

Deflated, she locked up the apartment and left for her mother's home. "Where have you been? We were terrified something had happened," her mother exclaimed. Having not heard from her, her mother and sister, Khaleh Soraya, had become uneasy and decided to visit their apartment. They arrived to the sight of boxes, and bags, and moving trucks outside. There, my father's family was rummaging through my parents' belongings—piling dinnerware, furniture and their rug into their cars. When they told my grandmother and aunt the family had left for good, they assumed they were never going to see Mom again.

Mom agonized over the decision of whether to return to him. She had two options: stay and raise her kids on her own in Esfahan, or leave for a foreign country with her husband. She sat quietly next to her mother and sister, eventually asking her mom what she should do. Her mom paused for a moment, took a breath in as if pulling back her tears, and said: "You have to go where he goes. There is no life here, in Iran, for you. A woman with two kids, no husband. There's nothing here for you anymore."

Numb, Mom loaded herself, her two kids and her single suitcase back onto the bus for the second time that week, this time saying goodbye to home for good. I listened to this story with my mouth gaping open, each detail deepening the grief and rage I felt for my mother.

"I'm so sad for you," I said as we stared into each other's eyes, tears welling up. It was gut-wrenching to see the story in its full truth, laid bare before me like an open wound that had never really healed. The excruciating reality of my mother being dragged away from her home, hanging on with both hands, begging to stay.

My mother said she'd held this story back because she hated how it made her look powerless, like a victim, or a woman at the mercy of a man and his whims. All she saw in it was a woman who had her life stolen from her. The one whose husband spoke for her. The one whose husband decided for her.

The one who was nothing and no one without her husband. She chose, for thirty years, to tell a different story. "We came here to give you all a better life," she would say. A familiar immigrant script that was easy to believe, but never felt fully honest. A "we" that concealed her lack of choice, her lack of meaningful participation in the journey. A "we" that concealed what my mother would later understand as abuse in their relationship. A "we" that maintained the goodness of all parties.

To my mother, it was a shameful story about herself. To me, it became a story about how catastrophic patriarchy is. That whether or not you're a dutiful wife, whether or not you're a good woman, whether or not you follow the rules, patriarchy is a catastrophic thing. A volcano daring to erupt at any point, burning down everything you called "home." And when you've had your home burnt down, you change, as Mom did. You exile all the parts of you that held power, presence and voice. Instead of asking why or saying no anymore, you become agreeable— shape-shifting becomes your language of survival.

I didn't know this story yet as I was leaving Yara's to move into my first apartment in Toronto, in a shabby salmon-coloured triplex in old Chinatown. Mom, certain that I was making a mistake, had fought tooth and nail to get me to stay. Now I wonder how much of this was her own trauma around leaving home. As if all the exiled parts returned in that moment, saying all the nos she couldn't say back then. Claiming power for the times when she felt powerless.

At that time, I anchored down into myself and what I knew to be true. I realized that leaving for Vancouver had been running away—from my family and from myself. But leaving Yara's for the last time was a movement of intention. Not towards home, per se, but towards a future and a home that were still in the making—my own making. I had to remind myself that though my survival felt like a tracing of Mom's, our stories were drastically different; and who we were, now, was also different. So I moved out. I hugged my mother and promised I'd visit.

Just before moving, I had started the job of my dreams, working in the anti-violence sphere with a team that cared about treating each person who walked through the doors with respect for their sense of dignity. Words like *justice*, *decolonizing* and *community care* were commonplace, evoking dreams of doing truly radical, meaningful work. I was a hopeful new graduate then, finally working in a building brimming with queer and trans community. At every hour, the space was buzzing with people pouring in for programming—everything from counselling to youth programs to housing support. Here, I was sure, I'd find like-minded individuals that felt more like family than colleagues.

I joined the team at a time of immense grief in the queer community. For seven years, men had been disappearing from the Church-Wellesley Village, and folks had been roaring about a predator on the loose. And when an arrest was finally made, they were grappling with the aftermath of that confirmation. With agonizing questions like what it would have meant for their loved ones had their suspicions been taken seriously sooner.

Loved ones had been anxiously looking for their friends and family, posting their faces from pole to pole on the Village streets. When I looked at the missing persons' faces and read snippets of their stories, there was something familiar about them. Some were refugees and immigrants with stories of fleeing home for better lives. Most were South Asian or SWANA, perhaps even Muslim. All with people who missed them dearly.

Hearing the stories of these men touched a wound within me. I wondered if they also struggled to bring the different parts of themselves together. If they, too, had to make hard decisions about which parts needed to be exiled and when. If they, too, struggled with the guilt and shame of it all. The un-belonging of being too queer for brown communities and too brown for queer communities.

Reading their stories reminded me of a time when I saw queerness as a utopia of sorts, especially as I was reclaiming my queerness in Vancouver. I believed violence didn't happen here—it happened over there, amongst the straights. Perhaps a survival story I told myself post-assault, wanting to believe in the safety of *something*. Over time, the cracks in that story became evident. But with this horrific tragedy, there was a painful reminder that yes, violence happens here, too. A whispered reminder to many who once joyfully walked the streets of the Village: *How safe are we really, here?* I looked to those I worked with for wisdom as they, too, grappled with what it meant to keep ourselves and each other safe. I suppose there was ease in sensing we were all looking at our armour a little differently, wondering how effectively it protected us.

Soon after I began this new job, my manager invited me to a meeting about a faith-based arts project featuring queer people and their individual stories. Its message was one that immediately moved me. Simply put: *You are valid* in the fullness of your identities. I wondered who would be willing to step up, into the light, for this project. There were ethical questions at play, for queer Muslims in particular. Like, what were the implications of your face being so visible? For many queer Muslims, myself included, the thought of being visible was terrifying. I called it being quiet queers, rather than closeted queers. We existed and had community and attended events and perhaps even had partners, but did so quietly, away from the gaze of others.

Some of the people at our organizing meeting argued that those interested in participating should be openly, boldly queer. I flinched at the term *bold* because it felt inaccessible to me. There was so much about being queer that was tied to being bold, a code word for "out and proud." To be boldly queer was to be liberated, to be courageous, to be self-loving. Though this wasn't what was said, what I heard in that term was that to be out was good, to be closeted was sad.

Most of my colleagues would be categorized as "bold queers," and truth be told, the more time I spent with them, the less queer I felt. These were people who seemingly lived so comfortably inside their identities, it made me question my own claim to queerness. They had stories from their baby-queer days of romping around the Village and drunkenly stumbling home. They had awkward moments of encountering their exes at work meetings or coffee shops because "the community is so small." They watched *RuPaul's Drag Race* regularly and quoted their favourite episodes.

I had to keep telling myself that I belonged here, though my expressions of queerness were more subtle. I was queer enough to be here, even though I didn't know who Bianca Del Rio was or what "sashay away" meant. Subtlety felt safer. Months prior, I had edged myself closer to "bold," participating in a youth radio show and almost immediately wanting to retreat. I had talked about being a queer Muslim and reconciling identities that, to some, felt opposing. Weeks later, I frantically emailed the host, begging them to remove my name from the episode. I spent days refreshing the page on my laptop until a different name appeared. I realized that I wasn't ready to be louder with my name, "out and proud." And perhaps I never would be.

Ironically, I barely felt like I could lay claim to my Muslimness, either. I had just started inching back into religious spaces, relearning what it meant to be Muslim. I recalled an incident back when I was first dating Ren, at twenty-one. They worked at a fast-food shop owned by Muslims. One day, Ren told them they were dating a queer Muslim, to which they responded, "She can't be a queer Muslim." When Ren asked why, they responded that you simply couldn't be both queer and Muslim. That queerness is *haram*, and so by that logic, a queer Muslim would never exist. Back then, I was young and impressionable, allowing other Muslims to dictate my claim to Islam. Now, reflecting back, I raged for that young, impressionable kid who thought she had to choose—and would go on to make painful, misguided choices.

I chose not to participate in the project. *I'm not ready*, I thought.

In subsequent months, I was delightedly immersed in advocacy work around sexual health education. The media so often pushed a divided view on the issue of sexual health, with Muslims and immigrants and people of colour on one side and white liberals, queer and trans people on the other. Though I feared visibility, some part of me felt hopeful that I—by virtue of existing across identities—could change the narrative. When management asked me whether I would speak to the media, I said yes.

Surprisingly, when I shared the news with my family that I was going to be interviewed, they were ecstatic. It was rare to see them excited about anything involving queerness or my advocacy work. Though, to be fair, I had stopped bringing it all up years ago. "That's awesome, dude!" Yara responded on our text thread, to which Mom added, "I'm so proud of you!" Dan and Yasaman chimed in, too, expressing how cool it all was. Their reaction was an abrupt change of tone that I welcomed.

On the day of the interviews, I arrived early at my desk and rehearsed the key messages meticulously. I practised intonation like I was a spoken-word poet about to hit the stage. When the event was set to start, Habiba, one of the managers, waved me over to an interviewer. "She's good," Habiba quietly whispered. The interviewer was a white woman from a liberal media source. Smiling kindly, she guided me to the hallway, where our interview proceeded. For the most part, I remembered our key messages and delivered them accordingly.

In the middle of the day, Yara sent out a message to our family thread saying Dan's family had seen me, on television and sent along pictures and affirming messages. Mom reminded me again of how proud she was of me, with a bunch of hearts. Even Yasaman cheered me on. It was the first moment when it really landed for me: something was changing in my family, in a big way. Never could I have imagined a moment like this, being celebrated for something so deeply connected to my queerness. I read and reread the texts like I had to drill them into memory before they were gone. Was this real? I wondered. After all these years, were they really on board with who I was?

Later that day, I sat in an empty, dimly lit office, barely "there." Being so fully visible to the media and public had suddenly overwhelmed me. I ruminated on the repercussions, catastrophizing all the things that could happen next. My eyes glazed over as I stared at the opposing white walls, disappearing into fuzzy thoughts and memory replays. I wondered if I had made the right decision.

I left work and zombied over to the subway station, scanning the streets for known faces to avoid. Forty minutes later, I arrived at the subway parking lot and slumped over to my car. As soon as I got into my car, I sobbed uncontrollably. I thought visibility would be a liberating, joyful experience. Instead, I felt immensely fearful and worried.

In Iran, homosexuality was not only a sin, but a punishable crime. One hundred lashes, or worse, death. For activists and advocates of human rights, it was especially hard to enter the country, the fear and reality of imprisonment always lingering. An anxious awareness that you were always being watched. That there was no way one could fly under the radar—though, as Mahshid had informed me, some people did.

I couldn't imagine a world where my family in Iran, like Mahshid's, would accept me as a queer person—or even tolerate it. My grief was a sign that I was nearing a pivotal decision in my life: to live quietly as a queer person, under the radar, or to be publicly queer, a vocal activist. The latter choice meant not going back to Iran, where the risk of punishment was too high, and I was too afraid.

There is no preparation for such a decision, I learned. No way to accept, with ease and grace, that you may never return home again. No way to explain that you *could* go home, but the cost is too terrifying a thing. No way to language a gaping wound that merely deepened each time I thought about it. Instead, in the car, I sobbed and I felt the weight of loss. I cried for the grandparents I would never see again. For the aunties, uncles, cousins I may never embrace again. For the family members I would never meet—those just arriving, and those still en route.

I yearned to see Baba Ali clean his herbs one more time. I yearned to hear him in his morning prayers—so loud, my mother still swears Allah could hear it. I yearned for the smell of gasoline and diesel in the streets. I yearned for the call to prayer booming in the streets. I yearned for the quiet moments of intimacy. My aunt exfoliating me in the shower, *sefid-ab* peeling away the dead skin from my back.

A couple of days later, I found the article and enthusiastically skimmed through it to find my name. I thought, *This is special.* I was just some kid from an immigrant family, and here I was with my name published in a news article. If there was any way to show my mother that her sacrifices mattered, this was it. Another part of me still struggled with regret. I wondered if the one-liner in the article was worth all of this.

For people like me, arriving has always also meant departing. And because we cannot be in two places at one time, there is always something we are leaving behind. There is always some degree of grief. I had not anticipated the way that arriving so loudly into my queerness would bring me to a departure I was unprepared for.

20

PERMISSION

Wanting to throw my sandal at anyone's head had become a simple cue that it was time to leave work. It was an impulse I had inherited from my mother after years of childhood discipline with a simple sandal, though one that I had never enacted except in my imagination. Mom was never a corporal punishment–type parent. In retrospect, it was almost comedic how she would suddenly slip off her sandal and chase us around with it, though her chase was just slightly quicker than her usual mosey. The sandal was often a chunky floral thing, flimsy and non-threatening when wielded by her.

There were other cues I had developed, too. I was now working at a small organization, continuing to work with survivors of violence. My left eye had developed a new twitch if I stared too long at the screen, or said yes too many times when I wanted to say no. My self-loathing inner voice would begin its checklist of fuck-ups, ruminating ferociously on everything I could have said or done differently that day. And there was crying in the bathroom stalls. When you're crying in the bathroom alongside other colleagues, who are also crying, you know it's time to go.

Often, the days would start well: no signs that things would go south and the instinct to throw a sandal would emerge. On this particular day, when Mo, my manager, approached me and asked if I wanted to work the weekend shift at an outdoor event, nothing in me was interested. Actually, there was a part of me that yelled, *Say no say no say no.* Yet I said yes.

It wasn't hard to say yes. Over the course of my years working at community organizations and non-profits, I had said yes to a lot of things. I said yes to weekend phone calls. I said yes to evening text messages. I said yes to staying late, to doing things that were well above my pay grade, to working overtime. The word danced out of my mouth like it had been rehearsed a thousand times. Like it was standing there, behind the curtain, just waiting for its cue.

In my first few months there, I had eagerly observed Mo, in awe of his dreams of radical community-based work with survivors, guided by principles of anti-oppression, abolitionism and collective care. He was passionate, often stretching himself as far as humanly possible. It seemed like he worked at all hours of the day—running to support community members in moments of crisis, then rushing back to his computer to finish a grant proposal, then to events as an organizer. I thought this was what it looked like to *really* commit to community-based work; you gave your *all* to this work.

At 8 a.m. that Sunday, I dragged my body out of bed and onto the streetcar, heading into the core of the city to an intersection I had strolled through hundreds of times before. Weekdays, it was always the same. Construction workers with their orange vests and Tim Hortons coffees in hand, their mouths motioning laughter against the harsh music of concrete drilling. Cars honking as they cut off cyclists; cyclists cursing at cars as they narrowly escaped death. Crowds of people exiting the subway station, their eyes glued to their phones as they traced their steps back to work.

This time, the intersection was utterly quiet. I made my way to the meeting spot across the street, where the event organizers were supposed to have left a box of items—water bottles, event t-shirts, lanyards. Two older men sat on the stairs to a coffee shop, eyeing me. White men with greying hair and peachy skin, loose-fitting jeans dragged to the ground, t-shirts oversized and faded. Between them, a cigarette passed back and forth. A quiet intimacy.

I walked over to our designated spot and looked at the open box that had been left. "I think that woman stole your shit," the men called out to me, pointing to a petite woman with short, fading pastel hair and oversized sweats. I watched as she sped away, arms full of a few water bottles and t-shirts. I shrugged my shoulders. "That's okay. Thanks." It wasn't really my shit, anyway.

I stayed in the empty spot on the sidewalk, waiting for colleagues to arrive. Nothing good ever comes from being the only woman on an empty street. Busy made me feel safe. Busy meant I could hide between cars, inside stores, amongst people. I could be invisible in busy. Here, on this quiet street, I felt naked.

I could hear everything. I could hear the clicking of bike gears as a man passed by and into the intersection. My eyes met his as he pumped the pedals. "Shit," I said to myself, noticing him circling back and now pumping his pedals straight to me. I had made the cardinal mistake, I thought. Made eye contact with a strange man, who now read it as an invitation for conversation.

"Hey, uh, you from around here?" he asked, smiling, still sitting on his bike, one leg stretched to the ground. The sun bounced off his bald white head and the thick chain around his neck. His tattoos peeked up from under his oversized sweats.

"I'm working here. It's a street festival," I said in my customer service voice, making it clear I was here on professional business, as if professionalism has ever saved any woman, ever.

"You Native?" he asked me. "You're pretty." My stomach started to turn as his body branched closer to me, his eyes observing every inch of my face. "No," I said with a noncommittal half smile. A voice inside me grew louder. *What are you doing—stop smiling!* the voice said. "You look Native," he said, continuing to stare at my face. The same half smile remained on my face as my body stiffened. He spent the next five minutes in a semi-coherent monologue explaining his work in music and how he had access to free concert tickets and would take women, who swooned over how good the tickets were. I was half listening to him, half listening to the voice in my head. *Why are you listening to this? End it here*, the voice said.

"I could get you tickets if you gave me your number," he continued. I oohed and aahed, softening any blows to the ego I might deliver. He continued to ask for my number, ask where I hung out, ask where I worked, ask for my number again. I politely explained that I was on the job and couldn't offer my number. Eventually, he hopped back on his bike, said he hoped to see me again and rode off. I hoped not.

The street was buzzing with more and more people. A few more colleagues had arrived with supplies, and together we set up a booth with pamphlets, buttons and stickers. In fact, I started to doubt that voice inside of me that said the day would be terrible. That was, until a woman appeared out of nowhere, reached into my long hair from behind and yanked it from my scalp before dragging me backwards, finally pulling out a clump of extensions and my own hair. She then pranced away, joyfully and quietly. My hair was still in her hand as she disappeared down a side street.

It was so abrupt, I wasn't even sure it had happened to me. I reached my hand to the back of my head, confirming the missing extensions, then walked back to the booth and pretended everything was normal. Straightened the pamphlets on our table and avoided eye contact with passersby. When the sting of people staring at me burned too deep, I turned away and started to cry. Eventually, I returned home, where I lay in bed for the remainder of the day, dazed and exhausted.

The next afternoon, G., my supervisor, invited me for a walk. I knew what it was about. News had travelled to her that I left the event in tears. I considered how to talk about what happened. Would I call it assault? Would I call it violence? Would I just stick to the facts and describe it as I experienced it?

Violence was a complicated word in this field. Amongst my peers, we pretended that the physical and emotional aggression, intimidation and harassment we dealt with wasn't real at all. Or that we weren't affected by the traumas and violence community members experienced constantly. We whispered about our experiences quietly to the colleagues we trusted, fearing that others would call us uncompassionate, overly sensitive or just not cut out for this kind of work. It was as if naming the harm we experienced would minimize or erase the very real violence experienced by the communities we supported.

G. inched slowly into the conversation, inviting me to describe my experience from the event. Her eyes widened, emphasizing her stunned expression. Her empathy felt brief, but even in its brevity, it soothed the embarrassment I felt from having been assaulted. She then told me that it was important to "get back on the horse" and continue working that event at its next iteration as well. It was a "tough love" approach. We sped so quickly past my feelings that I felt ashamed for having feelings about it at all. I'd hoped to be taken off the event, but that wasn't G. She was the kind of person who would shield you from physical harm, but not necessarily the type to hold your hand as you cried. I nodded along and agreed to return, not wanting to seem too soft or fragile for this work.

In the end, she asked me a question that was already taunting me: "Why didn't you fight back?" It echoed all through the hallways of my body. I wanted to tell her why some of us don't, but even I felt confused as to the reasons. If I couldn't even protect myself, how would I ever protect the community I was working with?

Amelia and I caught up over ramen noodles at our usual spot on Bloor. She was working as a counsellor with youth, which had always been where I'd imagined her. I arrived looking like a hollowed-out thing that had been pretending to be human for the past week, and almost passing. "Youth are mean," she huffed comically. "I think the salty eyes got me," I told her, implying that someone had jinxed me. We both laughed as she commented on how often I thought I'd been "salty-eyed." Especially lately.

I let out a big sigh and launched into all the things I was struggling with at work. The assault was just one piece. There was also the vicarious trauma, the culture of overworking, my overwhelming anxiety, the new twitch I had developed in my left eye. "Shit is hard," she commented as she slurped her noodles, knowing what the non-profit world could be like. Matter-of-factly, she explained that my workplace simply wasn't a set up for social work, at least not in a way that was supportive enough to staff. That it wasn't a personal failure; it was a structural one. One that, regardless of the heart of the organization or the empathy of those working there, plagued most non-profits.

It *had* occurred to me that it was a structural problem, but it was easier to believe it from Amelia's mouth. Non-profits weren't immune to perpetuating capitalist work cultures that valued overworking, compliance and "thick skin." "It's not a personal failure," I reminded myself.

I'd been so quick to claim my struggles as a personal failure, like if only I could be less triggered, or braver, or less emotional, it would be okay.

I was no stranger to workplaces with major structural issues; I'd seen those issues impact my mother during the years she worked at a garment factory. For as long as I could remember, Mom had worked at the same garment factory, as a packer. At seven thirty in the morning, each of the workers arrived at a dreary brick building in the suburbs with no signs, nothing to indicate anything inside. On days when Dad was in town, we would drop off Mom in the mornings with him. We were the lucky ones—we had a car that worked well enough to drive her there. Others would carpool, or walk the twenty minutes from bus stop to building.

Her best friend, Khaleh Sima, had worked with her. They both raged at how the factory worked them to the bone for minimum wage, barely covering their basic expenses. How they were expected to push beyond what they could physically do, carrying heavy boxes around, with no money to afford the physiotherapy they so needed. How they had no time for breaks, and even on breaks, were so fearful of job insecurity that they hurried back to their tables. And worst of all, how white women could enter their workplace as packers yet so quickly move up the ladder into head office and finance and HR.

Year after year, in the months of early spring, I remember her anxiously waiting for the call to find out if she had a contract for the year. Mom would call around to the people she worked with, asking if they had heard yet. She would hope and pray and pray some more that she would get the call. She would go over her last year and reflect on the facts: Had she been kind enough, had she said yes to enough overtime, was she pleasant to be around, did she take too many breaks? For over ten years, they called her back. For over ten years, I listened to her thanking them for the kindness of a job. And for over ten years, my mother bit her tongue and smiled at the very people who were burning her out and further disabling her. And after that, she remarried, gleefully leaving behind that factory job.

Every few weeks I took the subway to Finch Station, where my mother picked me up. After her divorce from Ehsan, she couldn't afford her apartment alone, so she moved into Yara's house. I had settled into my quirky apartment in old Chinatown, where she refused to visit me. Instead, I agreed to visit her at Yara's when I could.

The house was quiet that day. The two of us sat at a wooden table in the kitchen, sipping our chai. Her eyes beamed with pride as she asked me about my work. I struggled to muster up the energy to answer her questions, especially after an emotionally heavy week at work. I had spent most nights retreated into my room, barely able to string together coherent sentences. It was confusing; I was doing work that felt deeply meaningful to me, and yet I was barely able to keep my head above water. Normally my mother would comment on how exhausted I looked, but on this day, she refrained. Perhaps something in her knew that I needed gentleness.

"You know that I wanted to be a social worker?" she lamented, recounting the numerous times she had attempted to pass an English proficiency test in hopes of applying for college. With each failing grade, that dream faded into the distance, until it was gone for good. "But I'm so proud of you," she emphasized. The warmth in her eyes was like a balm for my aching, exhausted spirit.

These visits continued for months, where my mother poured me steeped tea and listened to me talk about work. She eventually revealed to me that she understood the hardships because she, herself, had worked with survivors of violence. My face looked stunned as I tried to process how this never came up between us. At this point, I thought I knew everything there was to know about my mother.

In the eighties, my mother had befriended an obstetrician who lived in her building in Esfahan. After she repeatedly described her desire to work, the obstetrician agreed to train her as a surgical assistant in secret. At night, my mother would leave her two kids asleep at home and travel twenty minutes to the hospital. There, she was trained to provide support during labour and birth.

Later, she was hired as a surgical assistant at a concealed abortion clinic, where she worked entirely during night shifts. "It was like *your* work," she said. Each night, she awaited the arrival of women needing urgent, confidential abortions. Many were survivors of sexual assault who arrived with terror and shame. Whether they were strangers or people she knew, Mom listened as they shared the intimate details of violent encounters, offering as much empathy as she could muster. To her, this was the most important work she had done in her life and she wanted to do it well. Not just for herself, but for the women who trusted her, too.

When I asked my mother why she left, she responded, "I couldn't do it anymore. What happened to them was horrible. It was *horrible*." She looked up as if trying to find the right words. "I just couldn't. My brain couldn't. I couldn't hear the stories anymore. I couldn't…" I looked at my mother, knowing exactly what she meant. To silently carry these stories home with you, until one day, you feel so heavy with all the stories of heartache and violence, you cannot keep walking. Not for lack of desire or passion, but rather, because humans weren't built to carry that much pain alone. My knees were shaking under the weight of it all and I wondered how long before I couldn't, either.

My mother lowered her gaze and said, "I didn't tell *anyone*. People would have judged me." After a heavy pause, I said what I thought no one had ever told her: "For what it's worth, I don't think your work was anything to be ashamed about. I think it was *courageous* for you to work at an abortion clinic, especially at that time. And I'm so proud of you for it, Mom."

Amani had been a long-time crush. They had short brown curly hair with a few grey strands peppered in, and eyes a shade of greyish-green I had never seen before. The first time we met, I introduced myself, to which they coldly said, "I already know who you are." Their dry response left me feeling uneasy and distant. Over time, they warmed up. I realized that sometimes they spoke in such a direct manner it just came off as rude to me, someone who softened every word and every sentence. I swooned over them in the office, though we rarely spoke to each other. It wasn't until a colleague's birthday that I put myself out there and started flirting.

After a week of exchanging messages, we began dating; around this time, too, things started to feel like they were on the upswing at work. It was new, and we weren't ready to tell our co-workers yet. So we developed a plan to keep our work and relationship life separate. We met outside after work so that no one saw us leave together. We didn't hold hands or kiss within a five-mile radius of the office. We stayed off social media, and we never talked about our outings. We wanted to keep it quiet, at least until we knew what we were. That was, until the incident we would forever call "the time we sexualized the workplace."

One night when I was working late and my office was quiet, Amani came to visit me during their break—already an atypical thing, given our rules and regulations for keeping work and relationship separate. As I was leaving, Amani leaned over and gave me a kiss on the lips—and just as they did that, our executive director sped past my office. I wanted to melt into the floor. "Did she see us?!" I asked repeatedly, feeling panicked. "I don't think so," Amani said coolly, unbothered by the whole thing. "She probably doesn't even know your name," they laughed.

The next day, a meeting notification from Mo—no subject—came through just as I sat down at my desk. My toes became sweaty and claustrophobic, scratching the inner walls of my sneakers. Even my clothes were too heavy. I thought I could feel my heart shaking, rattling around in my body like an unscrewed part. Something was wrong.

When I entered our meeting room at the designated time, Mo avoided eye contact. He shared that the executive director had alerted him to Amani's and my "canoodling" at work. I couldn't feel my face. I wished for an eject button to blast me to a faraway land, where I could be alone in my shame. His sharp monologue lasted probably fifteen minutes, though it felt like hours. He was shocked and profoundly disappointed in my actions. He explained that in the future, when he couldn't find me, he would wonder what I was doing. That I would need to rebuild a trust that was broken between us. That I had sexualized the workplace.

I was mortified to now be known as the "office canoodler." I apologized profusely to my executive director. And to Mo, who was so upset that for days he barely looked me in the eye. Along with the overwhelming shame was my increasing frustration about being judged by a single indiscretion. I worried that my history of sacrifices and hard work held no weight anymore. I saw myself as the office pariah, unsure if I would ever make it back into anyone's good graces again.

Following the incident with Amani, my work-related anxiety became unbearable. My colleague sent me to her therapist, Sarah, who ran her sessions over the phone—and quite frankly, it was easier that way. The anonymity of it all provided comfort for someone like me to throw all my shit on the ground and stare at it. Sarah was a white woman, and I generally struggled to trust white women therapists. Except her voice had the soothing sound of a yoga instructor's, lulling me into safety, and she was actually pretty good.

One day, Sarah asked me to close my eyes and imagine a younger me. And so I did. Me at seven years old: long curly hair, round face, stretched-out almond eyes. I imagined myself in a room alone, crying. My body folded on the ground, my hands covering my face. Then she asked me to imagine myself hugging that young, seven-year-old me. I wrapped my hands around her so tightly, I could feel her in my arms. And then I began to sob. "You can never be abandoned if you never abandon yourself," she said gently. It was a light-bulb moment for me. That I had spent so much of life abandoning myself for others—sometimes for comfort, sometimes for safety.

Appeasement, she called it. She explained that it was a common response to stress and threat, especially among women: to please others; to avoid conflict; to minimize our own needs and anticipate those of others; to shape-shift into more likeable versions of ourselves. The pull being towards keeping relationships intact, regardless of how unsafe they feel, or how much they erode your sense of dignity. This was the illusion, or perhaps delusion, of appeasement. That if we could sustain connection, it would grant us safety, security or belonging.

In other areas of my life, I had found ways to loosen or free myself from the grips of appeasement. Queerness was no longer something I was willing to minimize or sacrifice in exchange for cultural and familial belonging; nor was I so fixated on beauty standards, trying to shape-shift into the annual flavour of "pretty." But at work, I was still stuck in appeasement. I struggled to say no, to ask for what I needed, to speak up when I felt I was being mistreated.

My mother and I were similar in this way. She so often moved through the world with a smile as her sword, often sacrificing herself for the needs of everyone around her—even those who hurt and harmed her. Temporarily, it worked, too. Capitalism thrives on our appeasement, bread-crumbing us little rewards for our willingness to sacrifice our needs for it. But for many of us, if not all, we find ourselves on a hamster wheel, no closer to the safety and security we desire. My mother had few choices that would get her off the wheel, but I was realizing that I did. I was not my mother; I had the privilege of having more options, especially because of my education. I wondered what else I could do to loosen the grip of appeasement and do what I wanted: leave.

One night after work, I was so tired and hungry, I couldn't fathom hopping on a crowded bus heading east. Instead, I forked over fifteen bucks for an Uber. At eight in the evening, my head buzzed and my stomach thundered because all I'd consumed that day was a couple cups of coffee. I walked like I was buffering every few steps.

The Uber driver was an older immigrant man. Olive skin, with salt-and-pepper hair peeking out from under his hat. The wrinkles on his face telling stories of both happiness and grief. We bonded over our similarities. I learned that he was Arab, with three kids around my age, all of whom were his pride and joy. I told him my parents were from Iran and that we were also a family of five. That they came over in the nineties, too, with the same hopes and dreams. "All my kids are good kids. They got good educations, degrees, and live good lives now," he said, a light shining in his eyes.

"Why are you working so late?" he asked.

"I work a lot."

"Why?"

"I have a lot of dreams. You know? My parents came here like you. No English and a couple hundred dollars in their pockets. They sacrificed so much for me. I work so hard because I owe them. I want to see their joy when I accomplish big things. I want to make them proud."

"You know, I always tell my kids, 'I'm proud of you. You don't owe me anything. I'm proud of you. I sacrificed for you, yes, but you don't have to sacrifice for me.'"

I left the car in tears, so moved by this stranger who took the time to teach me something. That sacrifice does not demand reciprocity. Its beauty lies in the fact that it's an offering without promise. An offering for the sake of a desired, but not conditional, outcome. It's a gift, not a transaction.

Later that week, Mom called me and told me I was working too much, and that I needed to take care of myself. That I needed time to eat, and sleep, and take showers, and see friends. It was one of the rare times my mother spoke to me about self-care.

"I think a lot of kids of immigrants work like me," I told her. "We feel like we owe you for sacrificing so much. You came here with nothing. And for what? For us to live better. Have more choices—" My voice cracked and I paused. And then my mother said something that would change my course: "If you are trying to make me happy, you did. Whatever I wanted for you, you did. Whoever I wanted you to be, you became. Go, be happy."

I spent the next months looking for a new job, and when I found something new, I left.

21

POSSIBILITY

At my apartment in old Chinatown, I painted my room orange. It made me feel alive. In its quiet, I wrote letters to myself like an old lover. To all the parts I had exiled, the ones I had been unkind to, the ones I had abandoned. Ode to the twenty-one-year-old who etched *haram* into her body and prayed the gay away. Obituary for the brown girl who cosplayed white girls because she believed in the promise of whiteness. With every letter, a drawing. In every face, there was me. A hundred me's—my ribs, my left eye, a mouth daring to speak.

One day, I took a deep breath, said a prayer and started uploading the pieces to social media. The first was an illustration of three Muslim women with the words *Islam is not a monolith / Your queer Muslim identity is real and valid.* The more I created, the more I yearned to create. A few words became paragraphs became essays. The dislodging of words that had been stuck in my jaw for years.

Art, both writing and illustrating, became a way to free myself from the survival mechanisms that had taught me to disconnect—to minimize and even abandon myself. In ways, the page was a *sofreh-e nazri.* A spiritual gathering with myself, an invitation to feel as deeply as I wanted to feel, knowing I was right there with me. My art often feeling like prayer—one for myself, one for the collective. And always spoken from a place of truth. Over time, art wasn't a thing I did, it was a place I went. A sacred place where I could feel and heal. The parts I had long exiled were invited, too. They were no longer too shameful, too unsettling, too painful to be near. In the sacred place, I sat with the young queer who stumbled through her first love, the one who ran away to Vancouver, and even the middle school kid who pretended to be "Arman". And slowly the shame and pain became smaller and smaller.

Over the years, there had been a number of strange and often deeply offensive thoughts my dad had expressed on queerness. There was the time he declared that queerness was somehow contagious. That if I had queer friends, I would somehow catch the gay. And there was the time my mother phoned my father to let him know I was queer. "I didn't plan it, it just came out," she explained to me.

"Okay, but what did he say?" I asked, curious and oddly relieved that I didn't have to be the one who did it.

"He said it was because we let you hang out with girls so much that you became gay."

"What the hell, Mom? If I had hung out with boys, he would've called me something else."

We were at the point in our relationship where we could joke about my being queer, and it only made her slightly uncomfortable. Ever since I'd started creating art, things were opening up between us. Art had made me more honest, and regardless of how my mother felt about it, I was going to speak my truth.

"You know, there are rumours that Rumi was queer," I said to her.

"I know. Ooo, those days, many poets might have been," she responded, unsurprised and adding more information. It was confusing to hear. I thought, *How the heck did you gate-keep this very important piece of information?*

"Mom, I'm gay. These are things I'd wanna know," I responded.

"You didn't ask," she said playfully, shrugging her shoulders.

"I feel like you've really come along way. You used to struggle, and now look at you," I said to her, affectionately.

"Me? I never struggled," she said. "Always, I loved you."

I looked at her. I knew that my mother had struggled for years, but I sensed this was something she would never admit. It was as if admitting she struggled at any point was akin to saying she didn't love me, and therefore, she was a bad mother. As frustrating as it was at times, I held empathy for my mother. Just as she softened the stories of others, concealing their hard moments, she did that for herself, too. Perhaps she had to latch onto the joy, and the laughter, and the delight like a life raft. Otherwise, the devastation and grief would be too much; it would drown her.

"You know—I always knew you were gay. When you were born, I looked at your face . . ."

"And you saw gay?" I laughed.

"I just knew you were different," she said.

As ridiculous as that sounded, I felt proud of her. She was talking about queerness in a way that felt so far away from years before, when she'd whispered, "Don't talk about that stuff here." Laughing, even, with such warmth in her face. I didn't go on to tell her about the love broker and the tray with the dildo, but I could imagine a future where that was hilariously possible, and that was enough for me.

One afternoon, Amani and I drove to Yara's house. I had carefully selected Amani's outfit, and they had graciously gone along with it all, knowing how nervous I was. I spent time in the washroom meticulously blow-drying my hair, plucking my eyebrow and chin hairs, applying makeup, ironing my clothes.

Amani peered into the washroom to check on me occasionally before quietly backing away.

"Have you met my mom? She's going to question why I haven't done my eyebrows, or whether I do my laundry ever, or why my shoes look so scuffed."

In my eyes, everything had to be perfect. I could leave no room for my mom to think I wasn't taking care of myself, and that somehow that was connected to my queerness.

When we finally got there and walked through the door, my mom came rushing over to us, her slippers slapping against the ground. "*Salam!*" Amani said, which was one of a few words they had picked up. That and *khoobi*, which means "Are you good?" and *sefid*, which means "white." Mom pulled me in like she hadn't seen me in years and embraced me with a hug. The rest of the family walked over to the door, greeting us with a kind of warmth I was suspicious of.

Dory, now eight years old, looked up at Amani, trying to make sense of who they were to me. It looked like literal mechanical wheels were turning in Dory's brain. She spent the rest of her time staring at Amani and then back at me, staring at Amani and then back at me. Yara would later tell Dory that Auntie Rozie was like Carol from *Friends*, and she would understand immediately.

The next time I saw Mom, I asked her what she thought of Amani. "Nice face," she said. "I like Amani. Good name, too. Very easy." I asked Yara what she thought of Amani, and she liked them, too. Found them to have their life together, and to be kind in spirit. In fact, both of them liked Amani so much, their main reservation was that Amani perhaps was too good for me. That I needed to level up on my maturity to ensure I could keep Amani.

In the coming months, Yara and Mom became Amani's greatest advocates. They were there when Amani was going through a difficult time at work. Every time my mother called, her first question was: "How is Amani?" Every time I went over to Yara's house, she asked where Amani was. My mother would express great disappointment when I walked through the door without Amani. Sometimes I had to remind them that I, on my own, was good and exciting, too.

A few years had brought us a long way. It turned out that I had to catch up with the progress my family had made over the years. The inches, the baby steps, were now adding up. Queerness was no longer a thing that was tolerated so long as it was quiet and concealed; it was recognized and, sometimes, affirmed.

Yara had begun to move through changes in her own life. She was in a period of self-discovery, considering returning to school to pursue a new career. A huge shift, given she still worked at the office she'd started at during my early teenage years, having slowly moved up from a receptionist to a manager role. She was letting me in more, too. Reflecting on how her self-protective mechanisms affected those around her. And now on her third tattoo, a giant chest piece that peered through when she wore tank tops.

One day, I was at the dentist nearby Yara's workplace and decided to visit her afterwards. I quietly entered her office, taking a seat across from her as she finished her phone call. After a few updates about our general lives, she paused and looked away pensively. "I've been thinking about when you first came out as queer and why I responded the way I did," Yara said. She explained that it was a strange moment to reflect on because, up until that point, she felt she knew I was queer. There were conversations with her friends in which she'd said, "She'll come to it herself, eventually." Yet when the moment came, she felt so immediately terrified of the world I was about to navigate—a world that she knew was homophobic and cruel—that all she could see was fear. "How were you going to protect yourself now? You were *so* sensitive," she explained.

I understood what she was saying. That the reality of my queerness, of what I would have to face, had suddenly sunk in for her. That it was so immensely terrifying that she went into a protective mode that ironically did *not* protect me. "I knew I pushed you back into the closet. I saw it," she said.

I was acutely aware that some people never get this moment. To return to a moment of hurt with the intention to repair and heal. I held empathy for Yara. Where I'd had the privilege of space for self-discovery, for messily and clumsily seeking answers, she had been focused on keeping us afloat. She'd had to be protective for most of her life—of herself, of us as a family. A protectiveness that was so heavily shaped by her experiences as a new immigrant at nine, and as the eldest child. With no one to guide her, assimilation had become the shape of her armour, at least in part. It offered safety. It was effective, even if only temporarily.

Seeing Yara return to the conversation with such clarity reminded me of how deeply interconnected our existence is— across generations, across communities. That we are not just connected by our pain and traumas, but also our healing. It was living proof that in living so freely ourselves, we give others permission to live and feel their freedom, too. That in healing ourselves, we create space for others to do the same. I drove home with a single hope and prayer in my heart: that we could continue do that for each other and for the next generation of kids in our family.

22

HEAL

Every once in a while, I catch a whiff of something that smells so intimately like Iran, I want to chase it down the street, into another neighbourhood, into another city, into another country, across the ocean. I've learned not to chase it. Instead, I remain still as a rock, so as to not scare it away. Something about the smell of concrete in the sizzling humid heat of the city sun. Something about the herbs—the dill, parsley, cilantro—growing in planters on the falling-apart porch. Something about gasoline and motorcycles and old cars.

For a moment, I'm not here, I'm there. I'm next to my grandmother, who is passing me my *chai shireen* with her shaky hands, wearing one of her beloved knee-length tunics and her loose-fitted pants, matching in patterned deep reds and blues. I'm playing cards with my Amou Javid in my grandparents' front yard, his laughter in my ear and his voice saying, "Kid, you only coming once a decade?" I'm at the airport gates, my face buried in my Khaleh Soraya's black chador, gripping her like it will be the last time I see her. I wish I could liquefy home into a perfume, dab it on my temples, my neck, the insides of my wrists. Instead, I am always waiting for it to arise spontaneously.

There is a small house tucked into a side street in the west end of Toronto that I call home now. It's the smallest house on the street. Amani and I live here together, along with their child and our dog, Bones. On quiet days when I can hear the birds chirping outside and smell my *gheimeh* swirling in the air, I am reminded of what a gift it is to not only have a home, but one where all of me is welcome to exist. The joy and the grief, the love and the rage, the vulnerable and the protective. Sometimes, they co-exist peacefully; sometimes, they argue. The doors are always open for them, though.

I am reminded, too, of the gift of having a home that reminds me of home, that *feels* like home. Above the door hangs an evil eye, a present from my mother. On our coffee table, there's a leatherbound book of Omar Khayyam's poetry. There's a miniature painting hung above the bookshelf, a gift from my uncle. The bookshelves themselves, stacked with feminist theory, and queer literature, and progressive Muslim texts. In the kitchen, amidst our collection of spices, there's a bottle of pomegranate syrup, bags of dried herbs, and a mason jar of herbal medicine from my Khaleh Soraya.

In the back room, we have a growing collection of art. Some my own creations. Some from creatives we admire. Most queer. There's one freshly framed piece of art that sits on the floor, for now—a colourful portrait of an Iranian woman. It's the only surviving needlepoint piece my mother did in her twenties, as a new mother. It was once tucked away in a bin, but I had it framed, feeling the pull to protect it. I am scattered everywhere in this home, like home is scattered everywhere in me, now.

My grandmother, Khanoom, has since passed, and sometimes, when I smell something that transports me back to Iran, I think it's a sign that she is visiting me. She suffered a stroke and stayed long enough for my mother and me to say goodbye to her over video call. The two of us crowded the video frame, me yelling, "I love you, Khanoom. I love you so much," tears welling up. My mother, unable to speak, but trying to push through her tears to say her final goodbye. Just after the call, my grandmother passed away. A year later, my grandfather, Baba Ali, passed in his sleep, as he'd always wanted.

I still feel Khanoom's presence, at times. "Khanoom came to visit me," I'll tell my mother, the only person who immediately understands me. "Yeah?" "Yeah, I could smell her. She was here." "She visits sometimes," my mother says. It's a story I grew up with; that our loved ones, after passing, visit us from time to time.

In the mornings, I look at myself in the mirror, often amused by how much my face looks like my mother's these days. My hair, nearly identical to hers when she was my age, pregnant with me. The growing freckle on my face is exactly where her mole used to be. And the softness of my belly, now a thing that soothes me, reminding me of all the times I was held by my mother, my aunties, my grandmother—all who had soft bodies of their own. It's an intergenerational inheritance that keeps them near me, though we are an ocean away.

I sit on the couch, where the morning sun shines through the windows, warming the back of my neck. I sip my chai with a sugar cube between my front teeth, sweetening every sip. A blank page sits on my lap, but I don't think about the blank page. Truthfully, I'm not *here*; I'm rummaging through my insides, where rooms are so often overflowing with piles of clothing, scattered papers on desks, half-drunk mugs of coffee and a rug that desperately needs vacuuming.

Art is a kind of reckoning with the mess, the chaos, the underbellies and hard truths. I want to know the parts of us that bloomed in joy, just as I want to know the parts that emerged out of grief. To know the parts of us that have wilted over time. To know the parts that were exiled, not out of desire, but out of survival. Perhaps, in knowing ourselves more fully, we may discover another world where our closeness is defined not by grasping and holding, but rather by emboldening each other to be more free. We may even learn that owning our pasts and the people we've been will not break our relationships, as we so often fear it will; it will mend them.

ACKNOWLEDGEMENTS

To my mother and my sisters—you trusted me to share a story that was not just mine, but ours. I am infinitely grateful for your vulnerability, your radical honesty and your trust. Without you, this book would not have been possible.

Thank you to Don, for all the support and encouragement you've given me all these years. To Barb Besharat, for every coffee you brewed me, for every meal you made me, for every conversation we had. Your love and care throughout this writing journey was a gift at every stage. To my dear friends who gave me an ocean of space to process my feelings, who encouraged me to be brave: Emily Power, Naaila Ali and Victoria Watson. To my west-coast beloveds, Behshid Z. Foadi and Katie Boyd, for opening your doors to me so that I could return to Vancouver and write. For all the care and affirmation you poured into me while I pieced together those chapters.

Gratitude to my pal, T'ánchay Redvers, who opened the door to the literary world for me and encouraged me in. For always reminding me that our voices matter, our stories matter. To Stephanie Sinclair, for seeing a writer in me when I didn't. For making me feel like I belong in the literary world, too. To Rachel Letofsky, for believing in me and my writing. To the whole team at Knopf, for all the care and attention you offered this book.

And to my editor, Amanda Betts, this book would not be what it is without you. Because of your patience, your guidance, and your wisdom, this story deepened and evolved in ways I hadn't originally imagined. And for that I am so grateful.

AUTHOR BIO

Roza Nozari is a writer, artist and therapist based in Tkaronto ("Toronto") and known as *YallaRoza* on social media. Her work weaves together writing and visual art to share stories of wounding, healing and community. It invites radical reimaginings of our world, towards one more invested in collective healing and liberation. She is the illustrator of three children's books: Little People, Big Dreams' *Mindy Kaling* (2021), *Fluffy and the Stars* (2023) and *The Anti-Racist Kitchen* (2023). Her illustrations have been featured locally and internationally—from university campuses to sports arenas and pride festivals.